Trading Blocs, U.S. Exports, and World Trade

Other Titles in This Series

Westview Special Studies in International Economics and Business

Trading Blocs, U.S. Exports, and World Trade
Penelope Hartland-Thunberg

Among the numerous trading blocs that have appeared since the late 1950s, only the European Economic Community (EEC) has had a significant impact on the volume of either world trade or U.S. exports. Dr. Hartland-Thunberg points out that although the total trade volume of the blocs that involve less-developed countries (LDCs) has increased, this is due at least as much to a particular bloc-member's economic growth as it is a result of the trading bloc per se. Despite this caveat, she predicts that the rapid economic growth of these individual countries and the tendencies of corporations to invest or license in them could well make ASEAN and LAFTA increasingly strong forces in world trade.

Dr. Hartland-Thunberg is director of economic research at Georgetown University's Center for Strategic and International Studies. She has previously been a member of the U.S. Tariff Commission and the Council of Economic Advisors.

Trading Blocs, U.S. Exports, and World Trade

Penelope Hartland-Thunberg

Routledge
Taylor & Francis Group

LONDON AND NEW YORK

First published 1980 by Westview Press

Published 2019 by Routledge
52 Vanderbilt Avenue, New York, NY 10017
2 Park Square, Milton Park, Abingdon, Oxon OX14 4RN

*Routledge is an imprint of the Taylor & Francis Group,
an informa business*

Copyright © 1980 by The Center for Strategic and
International Studies

Library of Congress Cataloging in Publication Data
Hartlund-Thunberg, Penelope.
    Trading blocs, U.S. exports, and world trade.
    (Westview special studies in international economics and
business)
    Bibliography: p.
    Includes index.
    1.Commercial policy. 2.International economic relations.
3.United States--Foreign economic relations. I.Title.
II.Series.
HF1411.H328   382'.3'0973   80-16379

ISBN 13: 978-0-367-21188-2(hbk)

Contents

viii

List of Annexes

Preface

The impact of trading blocs, which have multiplied in number during the postwar years, on the volume and direction of world trade is a subject that has been widely ignored by both economists and foreign affairs analysts. Neglect by the former is perhaps more easily explained than neglect by the latter; in either case the neglect is not excusable. This volume, in exploring the impact of world trading blocs on U.S. foreign economic relations, fills part of the research and analytic gap.

The main body of this book is properly concerned with U.S.-European relations. Of special significance to one whose primary interest lies in U.S. relations with the Third World, Dr. Penelope Hartland-Thunberg's study emphasizes the reasons for the ineffectiveness of Third World trading blocs today. In so doing it underlines the importance of the quality of leadership and the dangers of bilateral jealousies and fears in the success of the developing world's struggle to improve its own economic well-being.

Michael A. Samuels
Executive Director
Third World Studies
January 1980

This study was partially financed by a grant from the Westinghouse Corporation, an indication of their continuing interest in U.S. international relations.

xi

Introduction

The spate of trading blocs that have appeared on
the world scene since the late 1950s has had -- with
one gargantuan exception -- virtually no impact on the
volume of world trade or the level of U.S. exports.
For the United States, its greatest impact has been
on the composition of exports, and that effect has
been marginal.
The exception is found in the European Economic
Community (EEC), which today accounts for more than
one-third of world trade (compared with a U.S. share
of 12 percent) to which one-quarter of U.S. exports
are directed, where over 40 percent of U.S. direct
foreign investment in manufacturing is located, and
with which more than one-third of U.S. licensing
agreements for manufacturing abroad have been
negotiated. Since its creation over 2 decades ago,
the EEC has been a dynamic force in the world economy
altering the geographic and commodity patterns of world
trade and U.S. trade. Prior to 1973, the impact of
the EEC on U.S. exports and direct investment was
magnified by the existence of an overvalued dollar
exchange rate.
The increase in the total trade volume of the
trading blocs which involve less developed countries
(LDCs) is at least as much the consequence of a bloc
member's rapid economic growth as it is of the trading
bloc per se. The two LDC blocs that loom largest in
world trade -- the Latin America Free Trade Area (LAFTA)
and the Association of Southeast Asian Nations (ASEAN) --
have as members some of the world's high-growth
countries. Investment and licensing activities in
these blocs have largely been directed toward politically stable, high-growth countries. The fact that
they were also members of a trading bloc appears at
the best to have been marginal in the decision of the
U.S. company to invest or license there.

Despite its recent and projected enlargement, the EEC is unlikely to be the dynamic force in the world economy of the next 5 years that it has been in the past. The stimulating effects on production, trade, and investment of its formation have about run their course; meanwhile, deep-seated problems of financial and structural maladjustment are plaguing Europe and the United States. Assuming that these maladjustments do not cause Europe and the United States to turn inward and pursue a highly protectionist course, the high-growth countries of the future will continue to be the high-income developing countries. Singapore, Thailand, and Malaysia will then make ASEAN an in-creasing force in world trade. Brazil, Mexico, and Venezuela, to a lesser degree, are likely to do the same for LAFTA. If a new generation of statesmen should take over leadership of LAFTA, its future could be considerably brighter.

Penelope Hartland-Thunberg

1
Trading Blocs: Their Impact on U.S. Exports and World Trade

Introduction

The long era of postwar prosperity that finally came to an end in 1973-1974 was marked by high rates of economic growth around the world, rapid technological change, and a sustained rise in the volume of world trade that was probably unprecedented in history. World trade, which expanded 5-fold between 1950 and 1970, was a leading force in the expansion of world production by 4.5 times The pace of world trade in the post-war era was about double that of the first quarter of the twentieth century, which in turn was roughly double the pace of the last quarter of the nineteenth century.

World economic expansion quickened after 1960. Between 1960 and 1972, world trade grew by an average rate of 7.9 percent a year, world GNP by an average of 5 percent. The heightened pace of international trade after the 1950s was the result especially of the completion of postwar reconstruction in Europe and Japan, the reestablishment of currenty convertibility at the end of 1958, the (General Agreement on Tariffs and Trade) GATT-sponsored reductions in tariff barriers that had accumulated through the six rounds of negotiations extending from 1947 through 1967, and the establishment in the Treaty of Rome, signed in late 1957, of the European Economic Community (EEC).

The birth of the EEC on January 1, 1958 marked the start of a proliferation of preferential trading arrangements that has pervaded world trade even since. In 1955, about 90 percent of world trade was conducted on the basis of nondiscriminatory most favored nation (MFN) tariff treatment; by 1970 MFN-based trade accounted for only 75 percent. Today that figure is probably no more than 50 percent (the computation has not been made since 1970). In fact, today, the United

States, Canada, and Japan are the only important trading countries whose products are dutiable in Western Europe. (Annex I lists those trading blocs officially recognized in the Tariff Schedules of the United States in 1978.* Annex II contains their vital statistics.)

Preferential trading arrangements -- embodying national policy that discriminates in favor of imports from one or a group of countries over those from other sources -- were by no means new on the world scene. The proliferation of customs unions and free trade areas during the 1960s, however, was in contrast to the basic philosophy and practice of the GATT era. The General Agreement, the basic purpose of which was to establish rules of proper conduct to govern international commerce, stated in Article I a policy of non-discriminatory, most favored nation treatment as the fundamental guiding principle for world trade. Other articles, however, stated permissible exceptions, notably Article XXIV pertaining to customs unions and free trade areas.

Outside of Europe, the proliferation of trading blocs was largely a response of the developing countries (LDCs) to the EEC model and to the frustrations of their perceived lagging growth. Despite the fact that as a group their rates of economic growth, both in aggregate and in per capita terms, were substantial, they were not high enough to diminish the chasm between their living standards and those that prevailed in the industrial countries. A free trade area, with or without a customs union, was generally viewed as a form of self-help available to the developing countries, especially if associated with an industrialization and investment program assigning a new industry to one of the members whose output would be marketable duty-free within the larger market of the entire bloc. Eleven of the present 13 trading blocs are in developing areas.

The motivating force behind the EEC was as much political as economic -- the vision that an economically interdependent Europe would lead to a politically harmonious Europe, thereby negating the possibility of another major war arising from intra-European conflicts. The EEC was planned as both a free trade area with a common tariff schedule for

---

*Although there seems to be disagreement among U.S. government officials about the content of the list and the focus of responsibility for changing it, the list embodied in the Tariff Schedule of the United States Annotated (TSUSA) is the only one published by the U.S. government. It is the basis for the data pertaining to trading blocs in this paper.

trade with the rest of the world and a common market --
an area within which the same price would everywhere
prevail for the same commodity or service. Although
it has yet to achieve a common market in any significant industry, as a customs union and free trade area,
the EEC has been enormously successful. Trade among
members (intra-bloc trade) rose from just over one-
third of their total exports before 1958 to over one-
half in the early 1970s just prior to the oil price
rise. Today it is just 50 percent. (Table AII,
Statistical Annex).

The decision of six major trading countries of
Europe (France, Germany, Italy, Netherlands, Belgium,
Luxembourg) to form a customs union and free trade
area, the exclusion of Britain from the group and the
apprehensions of the rest of Europe -- especially
Scandinavia, Switzerland, Austria, and Portugual for
each of whom the other six European countries represented major markets -- over the impact of the new
bloc on their export industries led the United Kingdom
to undertake the initiative in the formation of the
European Free Trade Area (EFTA). The seven EFTA
countries established a free trade area amongst themselves on January 1, 1960. They did not attempt to
unify their tariff schedules vis-a-vis trade with
the rest of the world.

Since the establishment of the EEC, the proportion
of world trade imported at MFN rates has declined
steadily. Trade under preferential tariff arrangements has grown more rapidly than world trade and in
addition, the share of the EEC (original six countries)
in total world preferential imports has increased.
Between 1955 and 1970, the EEC's preferential imports
(imports at less than MFN rates) rose from 17 percent
of the six countries' total imports to 65 percent
and the share of total world imports made up by EEC
preferential imports, from 2 percent to 16 percent.
Over the same interval, EFTA's preferential imports
as a share of world total imports rose from a negligible amount to 3.5 percent (which amounted to more
than 14 percent of world preferential imports).

Although the data have not been extended beyond
the year 1970, it is clear that the importance of
preferential imports in the world total has continued
to mount. The United Kingdom, Denmark, and Ireland
joined the EEC in 1973; at that time, the remaining
EFTA countries negotiated significant preferential
arrangements with the EEC which taken together mean
that the industrialized countries of Western Europe
now form a huge free trade area in industrial goods.
In addition, the EEC has set up preferential arrange-

4

ments with most of the Mediterranean countries and
with 52 developing countries in Africa, the Caribbean,
and the Pacific (ACP), most of which were formerly
colonies of the EEC members.*

*The ACP countries are not included in the U.S. list
of trading blocs although the Lomé Convention which
established the special relationship between the 52
(then 46) ACP countries and the EEC provides more
justification for such inclusion than the conventions
establishing some recognized trading blocs. The Lomé
Convention is a vast and comprehensive agreement on
cooperation in economic development that was signed
in 1975 to run for a period of 5 years. It was
renegotiated by the signatories for another 5 years
commencing in 1980. Its implementation has been so
sufficiently successful that some of the ACP countries
consider it a model for the future development of
North-South economic relations.

The most popular provision of the Convention is the
STABEX fund for the stabilization of commodity export
earnings. The aid program and the special measures
for industrialization have also been effective. The
EEC grants duty-free access to the products of ACP
with the exception of agricultural products and does
not expect preferential treatment for its exports in
return. The EEC has recently agreed to treat the
ACP countries as a single customs area for purposes
of establishing rules of origin; thus products
successively processed in more than one ACP state will
be eligible for duty-free treatment provided the value
added in all ACP countries together meets the pre-
scribed level.

The main complaint of the ACP countries concerns the
dilution of their preferences in the EEC market that
results from the EEC's association with Third World
countries and from its granting of generalized preferences to all LDCs. They also complain about the
EEC tariff structure which levies higher rates on
processed rather than on unprocessed goods, thereby
discouraging manufacturing in the ACP countries, it
is claimed.

Despite the generally favorable reception accorded the
Lomé agreements, EEC-ACP trade has grown less rapidly
than the total trade of either group. In part at
least this is due to the low level of development of
most ACP countries, their lack of infrastructure and
skills, and the specialized nature of their exports.

The only other trading blocs that have approached achieving total free trade in their internal exchanges are the Central American Common Market (CACM) and the Caribbean Common Market (CARICOM); trade in nearly all the goods that are exchanged among the members is duty free. The other blocs have done little other than exchange preferences for a few products. The ineffectiveness of most trading blocs among developing countries is traceable to great differences in the economic structure of members, to their having established no agreed schedule of intra-bloc duty reductions, and/or to political disputes and jealousies among members. Originally both CACM and the East African Common Market (EACM), for example, contained much promise for successful regional integration, but as a result of mounting political controversy among members in the late 1960s, each began to disintegrate. Today intra-block trade is smaller than before the formation of EACM. The intra-bloc share of CACM trade has declined since the "soccer war" of 1969 after which Honduras and El Salvador refused to trade with one another. For other members, it is still an effective organization, although the recent upheaval in Nicaragua puts its future in doubt.

Table I (page 6) shows the share of world trade accounted for by each trading bloc in 1976. In the aggregate, these blocs represented more than half of world trade, but excluding the European blocs they accounted for only 11 percent of world trade. Annex tables A-1 show the slow growth of intra-bloc trade in relation to total exports for each trading bloc.

The successful accomplishment of the basic goal of trading blocs, the stimulation of intra-bloc trade through the reduction of tariff levies among members, is perhaps the most significant indication of their effectiveness. Looking at the LDC trading blocs in the aggregate, the relative importance of their intra-bloc exports to their total exports rose from 7 percent in 1965 to 12 percent in 1975. In largest part, however, this increase is accounted for by the importance of petroleum in the intra-bloc trade of the two oil-producing blocs, ASEAN and LAFTA. Omitting these two from the totals, intra-bloc trade as a share of the total remained roughly constant between 1965 and 1975. (The data show an increase from 5 percent to 7 percent. See Notes to Annex III).

The huge increase in petroleum prices and also in certain commodity prices (e.g., groundnuts, timber, nickel, cocoa) between 1965 and 1975 served to increase the values of non-bloc imports and exports and thus to reduce the importance of intra-trade in which the

Table I

Exports of World Trading Blocs as Share
of World Exports, 1976

($ million and percent)

BLOC	Bloc Total Exports	Bloc Exports as % of World Exports
OCAM	5,312	1
ANCOM	15,229	2
ASEAN	25,984	3
CARICOM	3,224	.5
CACM	3,012	*
Council of the Entente States	1,970	*
EACM	1,646	*
EEC	328,182	36
EFTA	58,279	6
LAFTA	32,991	4
MAGHREB GROUP	7,383	1
UDEHC	1,889	*
CEAO	2,321	*
Total Trading Blocs	487,422	54
Total World Exports	906,000	

* Less than one-half of 1 percent.

Source: IMF, Direction of Trade

large commodity staples of the LDC's (except for oil)
play little role. The ineffectiveness of LDC trading
blocs is apparent in the relative level of intra-bloc
trade.

In contrast, the intra-bloc trade of the EEC and
EFTA has grown both in relation to their combined
exports and to total world exports. The combined
intra-trade of the European trading blocs rose from
34 percent of combined total exports in 1960 to 41
percent in 1965 to 45 percent in 1975. (It reached
a peak of 47 percent in 1973.) In relation to total
world exports, the combined intra-trade of the EEC
and EFTA rose from 13 percent in 1960 to 20 percent
in 1975. In view of the inflationary boost to the
value of world trade given by the 1974 quintupling
of petroleum prices, this increase in the relative
importance of European intra-bloc trade is the more
impressive.

Trading blocs, if effective, will generate an
increase in production within member countries as a
result both of the enlarged market available to producers and the stimulus this will provide to investment. The latter may be the indirect consequence
of expanding markets or the direct consequence of
bloc industrial cooperation and investment agreements.
The record of trading blocs in regard to cyclical and
secular output expansion is also mixed. Members of
the EEC and EFTA (almost all industrial countries)
did not suffer as deep or prolonged a decline in
output (GNP) as did the United States during the
1974-1975 recession. The relative stability of
Europe in these years is traceable in significant part
to their export industries (a much larger fraction of
GNP than is true in the U.S. economy). Both total
exports and intra-bloc exports of EEC and EFTA continued to grow in 1975 although exports to the United
States declined. Also, important in Europe's success
in maintaining export markets at that time was the
continued increase in the imports of certain rapidly
developing LDCs (e.g. Brazil, Singapore, Taiwan) whose
growth helped to sustain the intra-trade of the blocs
of which some of them are members. The two blocs
containing the most rapidly growing LDCs are LAFTA and
ASEAN whose intra-trade did not rise as much in 1975
as total imports and whose exports to the world
declined. In view of the fact that the EEC and EFTA
in 1975 were still benefiting from the trade-diverting
effects of the reduction in duties on industrial goods
between them, the evidence most probably should not
be interpreted as suggesting that membership in a free
trade area can help to stabilize cyclical swings in
income and production.

Long-term per capita average GNP growth rates of
European countries, (2 percent to 4 percent during the
years 1960-1976) while substantial for long-term rates
and for countries starting from a high level, have
been below those of the more rapidly growing LDCs
(over 4 percent). The latter are primarily to be
ascribed to the economic policies pursued by individual
countries rather than to the fact of their membership
in a trading bloc. It has frequently been observed
that the outstanding success stories among the LDCs --
Singapore, Hong Kong, Taiwan, and Korea, for example --
have been more committed to free enterprise and the
market mechanism than have been their less successful
brethren. This observation, however, does not deny
the importance for many of these countries of subsidies
and other forms of encouragement to production for
export. In addition, and of basic importance, by the
early 1960s they had succeeded in establishing an
integrated infrastructure and in building up a body of
skilled workers which provided the necessary foundation
for rapid growth. In every case their growth was led
by export and achieved, not through membership in a
trading bloc, but primarily through exports to the
high income industrial countries -- the United States,
Europe, and Japan.

In summary, viewing effectiveness in the limited
sense of achieving the basic goal of a trading bloc,
intra-bloc trade expansion, the EEC would rank first,
CACM second, EFTA third. For the first two of these
blocs, the share of intra-trade in total exports is
more than 20 percent; for the third, more than 15
percent. In each case, the percentage-point gain
in the share of intra-trade since bloc establishment
has been more than five. In the broader terms of
combined GNP, income per capita, manufacturing production, and various other indicators of economic
strength (Annex II), the EEC is also vastly more
powerful than any of the other trading blocs; EFTA
is second; LAFTA third; ASEAN fourth. The other
trading blocs are relatively insignificant in terms
of economic power.

Impact of Trading Blocs on U.S. Exports

During the years since the end of World War II,
U.S. exports have declined in relation to world
exports. In 1950 the United States accounted for
16 percent of world exports; in 1977 U.S. exports
represented 12 percent of the world total. Over the
past 20 years, U.S. exports have grown at one-half
the rate of other industrial countries. To an impor-

tant degree, some of this decline was inevitable as
the war-devastated economies of Europe and Japan
recovered their productive capacity. Indeed, U.S.
foreign policy during most of the postwar period was
directed toward bringing about such a decline. In
large ways and small, the United States undertook
foreign initiatives aimed at establishing economic
growth and economic interdependence around the world
in the interest of securing a stable peace. U.S.
support for Article XXIV of the GATT was based on
support for European economic integration and the
belief that trading blocs -- customs unions and free
trade areas -- would serve to create trade (as well
as to divert trade) and eventually at least serve to
reduce the average level of protection in the world
and thereby to increase the total volume of world
trade. Reduction in the level of protection, it was
believed, would more than compensate for the efficiency-
lowering distortion of world resource allocation that
would result from discrimination. Even if the criteria
of Article XXIV were scrupulously followed, such an
outcome would not necessarily follow.

U.S. support for European economic integration was
based on the assumption that an economically interdependent Europe would be a peaceful Europe. It was recognized that a European customs union would divert to
European sources products that had been supplied from
the United States and thus would entail an economic
cost for the United States. It was believed, however,
that the trade-diverting effect of the EEC would be at
least in part countered by the stimulus to dutiable
imports that would arise from expanded output in
Europe as member countries produced more of the total
imports of the bloc. The dominant goal, however, was
political -- to secure peace in Europe through
economic interdependence. Any net injurious effect
to U.S. exports that might be the consequence of the
establishment of a European trading bloc was viewed
as a small price to pay for peace. U.S. support (or
more properly failure to object to) trading blocs
among LDCs represented a reluctance, shared by other
developed countries, to oppose any initiative of the
LDCs which the latter believed would further their
own economic development.

In consequence, despite the failure of the Treaty
of Rome to spell out a common agricultural policy for
its members, and despite its provisions for dealing
with the association of overseas territories, the
United States acquiesced in consenting to the Treaty
of Rome as if it conformed to Article XXIV of the GATT.
Similarly, no objection was raised to LDC trading blocs

despite the fact that most of them ignored the GATT
criteria that substantially all trade between members
be duty-free. When the EFTA convention requiring free
trade among members except in agriculture and fisheries
was presented in the GATT, the precedent of the EEC
omissions was already established and no objections
were raised.

It is, of course, impossible to determine what
has been the impact on U.S. exports of trading blocs
because it is impossible to say what might otherwise
have happened, had preferential trading blocs not
been created. The evidence suggests that factors other
than the existence of trading blocs have been at least
partially responsible for the decline in U.S. trade;
that at least some of it would have happened even
without the existence of the EEC.

In 1950, Europe (EEC and EFTA) took about one-
third of total U.S. commodity exports. By 1960, just
after the birth of the EEC, this share had declined
to somewhat over 20 percent. In 1973, the year of
EEC enlargement and the jump in world oil prices,
Europe's share of U.S. exports had risen to 27 percent.
In 1977, it was 25 percent. In comparison, Europe's
imports from the United States accounted for 12 percent
of its total imports in both 1950 and 1960; for 8
percent in 1973 and for 7 percent in 1977. While the
importance of U.S.-European trade has declined for
both sides since the advent of trading blocs, the
decline in the importance of the United States to
Europe has gone further than the decline in the importance of Europe to the United States.

Given the postwar U.S. policy of encouraging
economic growth and world trade, European recovery
and economic expansion would have been substantial
and intra-European trade would have increased even
without the introduction of European free trade in
1958. Assuming that a Kennedy Round of tariff reductions or something at least similar would have occurred
without the existence of the EEC, trade expansion in
the 1960s and 1970s would have involved greater U.S.
participation in the trade of Europe and the rest of
the world. It seems likely that world resources would
have been somewhat more efficiently allocated among
trading areas, with less U.S. investment flowing to
Europe, that U.S. total output would have been somewhat
larger, although this cannot be proven. The Vietnam
war and the policies used to finance it, however,
would under the Bretton Woods international financial
system have caused the dollar to become overvalued,
with its consequent drag on U.S. exports and stimulus
to U.S. direct investment abroad. The overvaluation

of the dollar would probably not have been as large,
foreign investment would therefore have been smaller
and U.S. exports greater than was actually the case.
Insofar as the existence and expansion of the EEC did
involve distortion of world resource allocation, the
impact of that distortion fell largely on the United
States. This is because through a variety of devices,
the EEC members had effectively limited imports from
Japan, the other chief industrial competitor; imports
of the kinds of goods produced in Europe came largely
from the United States and the rest of Europe. The
EEC thus aggravated a U.S. relative trade decline that
would probably have occurred to some degree anyway.
But the existence of the trading bloc probably did
aggravate it.

Given the actual course of events, the factors
responsible for the decline in the U.S. share of the
trade of Europe are complex. Certainly the formation
of the EEC as a free trade area was an important
source of world prosperity in the 1960s. The trade-
creating effects may have been greater than the trade-
diverting effects in its aggregate impact on the world
economy. The most significant share of the trade
diversion, however, fell on U.S. exports. Because the
dollar was becoming an increasingly overvalued currency
during this decade, however, U.S. exports would have
lagged behind world export growth even without the
EEC.

At the same time, the overvalued dollar, making
imports and property abroad relatively cheap for U.S.
residents, stimulated U.S. direct investment abroad
beyond what would have been the response to changing
tariff barriers alone. Rising U.S. direct investment
in Europe was accompanied by an increasing outflow of
U.S. products (capital equipment, parts, materials)
as branches and subsidiaries of U.S. corporations were
established abroad.   In short, the overvaluation of
the dollar, exaggerated the impact of the EEC on U.S.
trade. U.S. exports of finished goods were increasingly
replaced by U.S. exports of "high technology" or "high-
skill items" -- machinery, components, semi-finished
goods, and such -- flowing from a U.S. parent to a
subsidiary in Europe. The increasing importance of
machinery and capital equipment in U.S. exports became
pronounced in these years. The share of U.S. exports
of manufacturing products accounted for by multinational
firms or a foreign affiliate rose rapidly.

Meanwhile U.S. balance of payments deficits caused
the government in 1965 to seek the voluntary restraint
of the U.S. business community in limiting direct
foreign investment in industrial countries to 90 percent

of the level of the early 1960s. The data suggest that the voluntary restraint program was effective. Direct U.S. investment in manufacturing in the EEC declined after 1966 (and that despite a statistical change that would have raised the dollar value of a constant level of direct investment after 1966. Table II, Chapter III).

Complicating the judgment about the importance of these influences was the divergent stage of the business cycle in Europe and the United States during the 1960s. Stimulated by the "guns and butter" Vietnam War spending program, the U.S. economy rose to a full-employment level of output in the late 1960s while much of Europe still had excess capacity.* More rapidly rising income in the United States made the domestic market more attractive, tended to put a drag on U.S. exports and to counter somewhat the attractions of investment in Europe.

Judgments will vary about the relative importance of these different factors as they have acted to propel U.S. exports both up and down. As stated earlier, we believe that lagging U.S. export performance during the 1960s is to be ascribed in important part to the increasingly overvalued dollar and to the booming domestic economy at a time of excess capacity in Europe and Japan. Overall during the 1960s, the aggregate impact of the EEC on U.S. exports was probably negative, with trade-creating effects aided by other influences partially countering trade-depressing effects. It was, however, one additional factor depressing U.S. exports.

During the 1970s, U.S. export performance has continued to lag but for a somewhat different mix of reasons. Except for a brief period at the start of the decade, business cycle phases have continued to diverge in Europe and the United States with continued significant impact on the U.S. trade performance. In addition, price-level movements have been wildly divergent during the 1970s and fluctuating exchange rates have sometimes under -- sometimes over -- compensated. Nonetheless, the expansion of the EEC from six to nine members in 1973 and especially the concomitant expansion of the EEC's preferential relations with remaining EFTA members (and to a lesser degree with developing countries) appear to continue to have been at least marginally negative in their aggregate effect on U.S. exports to date.

---

* OECD Occasional Studies The Measurement of Domestic Cyclical Fluctuations, July 1973.

Since the 1973 EEC enlargement, Europe has suffered cyclical recession and excess capacity. This fact served to depress U.S. direct investment in Europe somewhat. In addition, a more realistically valued dollar removed some of the stimulus to U.S. investment in Europe that had existed earlier and its boot to U.S. exports. At the same time, the more realistically based dollar also meant that the exchange rate would no longer be a drag on exports (as it had been in the 1960s) although these effects appear with a lag. Thus the impact of trading bloc enlargement on the volume of U.S. exports and their commodity composition was not subject to the exaggerating effects of exchange rate overvaluation that had existed in the earlier decade. U.S. exports at the same time, however, tended to be depressed by cyclical desynchronization and the trade diverting effects of trading blocs. Although exports were somewhat stimulated by the trade-creating effects of direct foreign investment in the bloc, that stimulus was diluted by relatively greater prosperity in the United States than in Europe. (Existence of excess capacity in Europe has caused European producers to seek more aggressively markets in third world countries. This they have been doing successfully in Latin America and Asia which has been a further factor depressing U.S. exports.) Between 1973 and 1977, total EEC imports increased by 80 percent; intrad-trade by 72 percent and imports from the United States by 60 percent; at the same time, EFTA's imports from the world also increased 80 percent; from intra-trade by 62 percent; from the U.S. by 87 percent (but EFTA imports from the United States rose from 5½ percent of total imports to only 6 percent of the total). Clearly the extension of free trade in industrial goods between the EEC and EFTA that accompanied enlargement of the EEC has been a more important source of trade and investment stimulation for Europe than was the concurrent expansion of the EEC from six to nine members.

The extension of free trade in industrial goods among EEC and EFTA members in effect creates an additional trading bloc and offers new opportunities for expanding European markets. Since intra-European duties on industrial goods only reached the zero level in 1978, the full effects of the new free trade area may not yet show up in the trade or investment data. The merging of these two blocs by the elimination of duties on industrial goods between them will probably provide some additional stimulus to trade and investment in Europe but the addition will be marginal. The countries involved are small in relation to the EEC. The elimination of tariffs between them essentially

recognizes and extends the free trade that had prevailed between the United Kingdom, Ireland, and Denmark,
before they joined the EEC, and the rest of EFTA. What
is new is free trade in industrial goods between the
smaller EFTA countries and the six original EEC members.

Both the EEC and EFTA have been operating individually as free trade areas for about 2 decades. The
impact of their revised tariff structures is by now
nearly complete. It seems likely, therefore, that
the trade-diverting impact of European trading blocs
on U.S. exports is largely past, that in the future
their effect on U.S. exports will be negligible.

The ineffectiveness of most LDC trading blocs to
date means that the impact on U.S. exports has been
small. The decline in the U.S. share of LAFTA trade
during the early 1960s was more a result of the
increasing competitiveness of Europe and Japan as they
completed their postwar recovery than it was the
replacement of the United States by LAFTA markets. In
the late 1960s and early 1970s, LAFTA's imports from
Europe and Japan were stimulated by the overvalued
dollar (as were U.S. imports) because of its members'
belonging to the dollar bloc. LAFTA's share of members'
exports rose from an average of 8 percent in the late
1950s to 13 percent in recent years. About half of this
increase came after 1973 when higher oil prices
helped to raise the intra-bloc totals.

During the 1970s, LAFTA has been the most effective of the LDC trading blocs in promoting economic
development and industrialization via regional integration. Between 1970 and 1976, manufactured goods rose
as a share of the total exports to LAFTA markets of
most member countries. For Argentina, the increase
was from 27 percent to 29 percent; for Brazil, from 33
percent to 46 percent; for Colombia, from 4 percent
to 8 percent. The exception was Mexico where manufactures remained at 17 percent of total exports to
LAFTA. For Mexico, however, over the same period
exports of manufactures to the United States rose
from 24 percent to 47 percent of the total. For
Brazil also, the U.S. market for manufactured exports
rose, from 16 percent to 22 percent. Thus although
its impact on U.S. exports has been slight, LAFTA has
played a small role in the expansion of manufactured
exports of its members. Given the attraction of Brazil
as a site for U.S. direct investment in manufacturing
since the late 1960s, it seems likely that U.S. industry has shared in this expansion.

To sum up, lagging U.S. export performance since
1960 is to be explained primarily in terms of U.S.
domestic economic policy, increasing competitiveness

of Europe and Japan, and unrealistic exchange rates and only secondarily in terms of the growth of preferential trade in Europe or elsewhere. The distorting effects of European trading blocs on world trade and on the volume and composition of U.S. exports are largely in the past since the adjustment of production in Europe to the reality of trading blocs seems to be nearly complete.

2
Direct Investment in Manufacturing in Trading Blocs

Introduction

Some trading blocs function in addition as an instrument for regional economic integration; in these cases they are likely to articulate policies toward investment, although not necessarily toward foreign investment. Other trading blocs are concerned only with trade and do not attempt to influence or regulate directly either national or foreign investment. In these cases policy toward foreign investment is that of the members individually and may vary considerably from one part of the bloc to another. For a number of years De Gaulle's France, for example, selectively limited direct foreign investment in France while his neighbors in the EEC adopted no such restrictions.

The establishment of a free trade area, however, if reasonably comprehensive, will by itself influence investment patterns within the trading bloc. Production facilities will be established in those parts of the area where prospective unit costs are least. If one member country places more rigorous controls on investment -- domestic or foreign -- than another, its growth will lag, its share of intra-trade will decline. The full potential benefits from a free trade area will be realizable only if no member limits the mobility of capital. This implies a common bloc-wide policy toward foreign investment. In fact, most trading blocs aim toward such a common policy although few have attempted to achieve it.

Although no foreign investment code has been articulated by the EEC or EFTA for adoption by their members, the EEC Commission has initiated a number of proposals in the industrial field which have two main objectives: to eliminate the remaining barriers to intra-EEC trade and investment and to promote European-based multinational enterprises able to compete effectively with U.S.-based firms established in

Europe. The Commission has explicitly stated that national measures undertaken in pursuit of these objectives should apply without discrimination between Community and third-country enterprises. In its own activities, the Commission appears to have applied these standards of nondiscrimination. In general, most European governments have been at least neutral toward foreign investment, although most, in maintaining currency controls, do possess the ability to influence the size and direction of foreign investment.

The Andean Common Market members have gone further than other LDC trading blocs in attempting to implement a common foreign investment policy. Despite a comprehensive foreign investment code adopted by ANCOM in July, 1971 ("Decision 24"), it is in fact being implemented in widely different degress by bloc members. Only one member, Venezuela, adheres to the criteria of Decision 24 completely. None of the other LDC trading blocs has adopted a foreign investment code, although several aim to do so eventually.

Decision 24 attempts to regulate foreign direct investment in order to make more of the benefits available to the host country. Decision 24 objectives appear to embody the perceptions of many LDCs about the past inequities of foreign investment in general and of the activities of the large multinational companies in particular. Its requirements for local participation are rigorous. That more such investment codes have not been adopted by the LDC trading blocs is probably due to the chastening experience of the world's recent recession.

When Decision 24 was adopted, commodity prices were rising around the world; Europe, the United States, and Japan were all in the expansion phase of the business cycle which for the first time in 20 years was synchronized throughout the industrial countries. Demand for raw materials was growing rapidly and the LDCs were prospering. The success of OPEC 2 years later, in wrenching upward its members' foreign exchange receipts from oil, added to the LDCs aspirations toward greatly revised conditions of foreign investment. Since the collapse of many commodity markets in 1975, however, LDCs have taken a more realistic attitude toward the degree to which foreign investment can be regulated without causing it to disappear completely. They still want larger returns than they were able to negotiate in the past, however, and recently several LDCs have hired skilled negotiators from the United States and elsewhere to advise them in actual bargaining over the terms of investment with large multinationals. The results from their point of view have been highly satisfactory. This practice is likely to spread.

Impact of Trading Blocs on
U.S. Direct Involvement in Manufacturing

Most LDCs are underdeveloped in their statistical collection and processing systems. Their economic
data are generally low in quality and scant in quantity. This weakness is especially obvious in their
statistical series relating to international financial
transactions. The less developed countries do not
attempt to collect data on total foreign direct investment, to say nothing of data relating specifically
to investment in manufacturing from one foreign source.
U.S. data are, of course, much better only for the
countries that have been the major recipients of U.S.
capital. Data on U.S. direct investment in manufacturing is available only for the EEC countries; for
the rest of the trading blocs availability is spotty.
For Africa, it is nonexistent (lumped together with
other countries into a comprehensive "all other"
category).
        The comparison between aggregate U.S. direct
investment and direct investment in manufacturing
for the three EFTA countries for which both series
are available (Tables III and IV) is instructive.
Investment in manufacturing represented 13 percent
of total U.S. direct investment in Switzerland, 18
percent in Norway, and 53 percent in Sweden for the
period 1966-1977. These are the magnitudes one would
expect from a general knowledge of the nature of the
three economies. Moreover, even in Switzerland where
the absolute amounts were largest, the amount flowing
to manufacturing for the 12-year interval was an
average of only $50 million a year; for Norway, the
average was $20 million; for Sweden, $38 million.
Where the data is not available, the amounts lost in
"all other" clearly are small.
        The 1960s were the salad days of the U.S. multi-
national corporation. U.S. businesses went abroad in
increasing numbers in every industry, manufacturing
included. While they truly circled the globe, the
concentration in Europe was heavy. In 1960, 58 percent of U.S. direct investment in manufacturing went
to Europe; in 1973, 49 percent: in 1977, 53 percent.
        U.S. manufacturing enterprises that extended
their operations abroad were typically U.S. growth
industries whose products were characterized either
by high technology or rapid technological or product
changes or both. Research at the Harvard Business
School under the direction of Raymond Vernon has
illuminated the causes and consequences of this flow

of U.S. capital and technology abroad. A summary of
the evidence collected in that effort states:

> U.S. production tended to exceed its consumption
> in the early stages following the introduction of
> a new product. The characteristic pattern for
> the United States at that stage was to build up
> exports to other countries, mainly to Canada
> and Western Europe. However, at some point,
> U.S. enterprises began to sense the need for
> local production: partly in response to the
> appearance of local imitators, partly out of
> fear that imitation would soon begin. There-
> fore, exports tended to diminish; indeed in a
> few cases such as in various lines of office
> machinery, the net export pattern turned to
> net imports. Even when the United States did
> not become a net importer, however, U.S. enter-
> prises began to use their European subsidiaries
> for the provisioning of third country markets
> of the Commonwealth, Asia, and Africa. *

The main motivation leading to production abroad
was thus found to be a perceived threat to an export
market of a U.S. firm arising from local competition.
Such a perception of threat could arise from the
likelihood of new restrictions on imports from the
United States. A free trade area places competitors
located within its boundaries at an advantage over
those on the outside.
During the 1960s, U.S. enterprise was clearly
reacting to the new competitive realities brought
about by the elimination of tariffs on intra-EEC
trade (See Table II). It was reacting also to the
fact that EEC-based industry would receive preferential tariff treatment in the associated overseas
countries. Until 1976, the ACP countries (actually
their predecessors) as well as associates in Europe
and the Middle East, were required by the EEC to
grant "reverse preferences" on imports from the
Community. These reverse preferences are no longer
required in the Lomé Convention, but in fact they
still exist in a number of cases. U.S. industry
was also reacting to high growth rates in Europe,

---

* R. Vernon, "Economic Consequences of U.S. Foreign
Direct Investment," (testimony submitted to the
Commission on International Trade and Investment
Policy, Williams Commission), United States Inter-
national Economic Policy in an Interdependent World,
Papers, Washington, July 1971.

Table II

U.S. Direct Investment[1] in Manufacturing in

The EEC Countries, 1950-1977

(Millions of dollars)

Year	Total[2] 9	Total[2] 6	Belgium & Lux- embourg	France	Germany	Italy	Nether- lands	Den- mark	Ire- land	United Kingdom
1950	126	51	8	21	17	4	2	*	**	75
1951	134	62	19	23	13	5	1	*	**	73
1952	119	44	6	21	12	5	1	*	**	75
1953	117	41	6	17	10	4	3	*	**	76
1954	151	55	8	17	15	9	6	2	**	94
1955	179	65	7	22	26	6	5	-1	**	115
1956	259	118	13	26	58	14	7	3	**	138
1957	270	105	18	25	48	8	5	*	**	165
1958	253	129	10	29	60	20	10	1	**	123
1959	414	163	1	47	81	24	11	1	**	250
1960	834	286	16	60	148	42	20	*	**	548
1961	387	235	28	64	110	26	18	5	**	147
1962	565	364	-3	111	205	29	23	-1	**	202
1963	637	424	48	172	142	39	22	3	**	210
1964	889	607	71	138	192	157	41	2	**	280
1965	935	599	73	192	229	58	48	5	**	331
1966	954	609	105	129	250	90	95	6	1	338
1967	783	582	84	85	222	85	106	8	14	179
1968	883	466	111	47	190	33	85	2	23	392
1969	1,287	912	77	160	431	143	100	5	37	333

1970	1,290	837	176	247	99	88	127	8	27	418
1971	1,718	1,175	184	294	436	203	57	-2	28	517
1972	1,717	1,330	143	329	534	154	180	*	53	334
1973	2,949	1,972	253	499	804	263	152	21	66	840
1974 3/	2,694	1,831	325	482	370	305	348	16	105	742
1975	1,586	1,228	187	426	508	33	74	**	**	249
1976	2,254	1,779	200	33	1,324	149	123	33	171	222
1977	2,328	773	278	144	283	86	230	11	146	1,150

* Between -$500,000 and +$500,000.

** Not Available.

1/ Defined as equity and intercompany account outflows to and reinvested earnings in foreign affiliates of U.S. corporations which held at least 25 percent ownership interest prior to 1966 and 10 percent interest in all subsequent years.

2/ The original six members formed the EEC by an agreement which became effective on January 1, 1958; Britain, Ireland, and Denmark were subsequently admitted for membership as of January 1, 1973.

3/ See Note 3 at end of Chapter.

Source: Survey of Current Business

rising incomes and rapidly expanding markets there.
And of prime importance to U.S. enterprise, an increasingly overvalued dollar made the calculus of
earnings from production in Europe vs. earning from
exports to Europe from the United States increasingly
favorable to operations abroad. Not only were imports becoming cheaper in dollars, but foreign land,
buildings and labor were becoming cheaper also.

Among the EFTA countries, Switzerland, Norway,
and Sweden have attracted most interest from U.S.
multinationals. Over 90 percent of U.S. direct investment in EFTA, 1966-1977 went into these three,
with Switzerland alone attracting over 60 percent
of the total. Most of the remainder was accounted
for by Austria. Assuming that U.S. investment in
manufacturing in EFTA is proportional to U.S. manufacturing investment in relation to the total in
Switzerland, Norway, and Sweden (19 percent of total
direct investment), it would amount to less than $1.5
billion for 1966-1977. This compares with over $20
billion in manufacturing in the EEC for the same
period. The dominance of the EEC in the interest of
U.S. multinationals is evident. (Tables II and V)

The combination of factors favoring U.S. direct
investment in manufacturing in Europe lasted until
1972-1973. Prosperity then came to an end in Europe
and, since 1975, the European recovery has not been
as vigorous as that in the United States. The
effects on U.S. direct investment are apparent in
Tables II and III. After 1974, both domestic and
foreign investment in Europe were further depressed
by the growing political strength of leftist parties,
especially in France, Italy, and Germany, and the
likelihood that the center-left coalitions that had
ruled since the end of the war would come to an end.

The realignment of exchange rates in 1973 and
the inauguration of managed floating rates has made
the dollar a more realistically valued currency. The
elimination of overvaluation in the dollar by itself
would make the choice between exports from the United
States or production in Europe more favorable to U.S.
exports than it had been. Imports have become more
expensive in dollars since 1973 and so have foreign
productive assets.

By the same token, the realignment of exchange
rates which caused European currencies to appreciate
in terms of the dollar has made dollar assets relatively cheap for Europe and Japan. The results show
up in the rapid rise of foreign direct investment in
the United States. Such currency realignments are
also partially responsible for the enhanced role of

Table III

U.S. Direct Investment[1] in Manufacturing
Three EFTA Countries: 1950-1977
(Millions of dollars)

Year	Norway	Sweden	Switzerland
1950	*	2	2
1951	1	4	2
1952	1	2	*
1953	2	2	1
1954	2	7	2
1955	1	1	2
1956	1	1	4
1957	1	1	3
1958	1	1	13
1959	1	9	29
1960	3	-21	22
1961	2	9	13
1962	2	2	9
1963	4	13	19
1964	5	9	26
1965	14	14	17
1966	8	12	49
1967	12	22	77
1968	11	51	23
1969	17	54	49
1970	13	40	41
1971	9	64	-35
1972	11	38	13
1973	25	44	211
1974	38	121	94
1975	18	33	114
1976	33	24	33
1977	48	-45	-55
TOTAL 1966-77	243	458	614
	18%	55%	13%

*   Between -$500,000 and +$500,000.

1/ Defined as equity and intercompany account outflows
to and reinvested earnings in foreign affiliates of
U.S. corporations which held at least 25 percent
ownership interest prior to 1966 and 10 percent
interest in all subsequent years.

Source: Survey of Current Business.

Table IV

U.S. Direct Investment[1] (in all Industries) in
The EFTA Countries: 1966-1977[2]
(Millions of dollars)

Year	Austria	Finland	Iceland	Norway	Portugal	Sweden	Switzerland	TOTAL EFTA
1966	16	9	2	27	6	52	204	316
1967	6	1	1	16	7	72	158	261
1968	10	3	*	24	8	87	132	264
1969	15	6	*	25	24	91	279	440
1970	21	8	*	37	15	61	250	392
1971	28	7	*	23	21	72	209	360
1972	26	13	*	32	13	30	157	271
1973	12	9	1	105	31	100	806	1,064
1974	32	23	1	246	43	182	888	1,415
1975	61	29	*	77	-13	77	485	716
1976	34	14	-1	366	10	32	603	1,058
1977	52	2	*	411	4	9	553	1,031

* Between -$500,000 and +$500,000.

1/ Defined as equity and intercompany account outflows to and reinvested earnings in foreign affiliates of U.S. corporations which held at least 25 percent ownership interest prior to 1966 and 10 percent interest in all subsequent years.

2/ Data for years prior to 1966 not available.

Source: U.S. Department of Commerce, unpublished files.

Table V

U.S. Direct Investment (all Industries) in
EFTA, including Ireland, Denmark, and United Kingdom
1966-1977
(Millions of dollars)

Year	Ireland	Denmark	United Kingdom	TOTAL
1966	22	25	477	840
1967	21	48	519	849
1968	33	-68	686	1,051
1969	39	58	535	1,072
1970	19	56	893	1,360
1971	30	-3	1,113	1,500
1972	55	23	492	841
1973	76	106	1,409	2,655
1974	126	176	1,460	3,186
1975	174	-57	1,429	2,253
1976	235	104	1,793	3,190
1977			536	1,595

Source: Survey of Current Business.

Europe and Japan in investment in other parts of the
dollar-area, Latin America especially. The high value
of the DM in terms of the dollar gives the German con-
cern a competitive advantage in negotiating a joint
venture, an extension of credit or an equity position
in Brazil. Outside of the dollar area, in the ACP
countries U.S. enterprise may be at a double competitive disadvantage: exports from the United States
may encounter discriminatory tariffs as compared with
those faced by a European exporter and the direct
investment dollar now buys less in comparison with
European currencies both in Europe and in European
currency areas than was true.

In 1973, the size of the EEC customs union was
enhanced by the addition of the United Kindgom,
Ireland, and Denmark. The size of the EEC was further
enlarged by the de facto inclusion of the rest of
EFTA into the EEC for trade in industrial commodities.
While some additional stimulus to Europe's trade and
production probably was derived from this enlargement,
its impact on U.S. investment was overwhelmed by other
events. Except for the United Kingdom, the countries
involved are relatively small as is their volume of
trade. The United Kingdom, because of the similarity
of languages, laws and customs, has always been
favored as a locus for U.S. enterprise in Europe;
much of the impact of the EEC enlargement on U.S.
direct investment in Europe had probably already
taken place before 1973.

The admission of Ireland to the EEC did promote
an influx of U.S. direct investment in manufacturing,
especially in labor-intensive lines. Ireland's low
wages and special incentives for foreign investment
caused its level to rise from negligible amounts in
the early 1960s to nearly 4 percent of the total
flowing into the nine EEC countries during 1966-1977.

Thus the combination of factors that during the
1960s tended to favor the choice of direct investment
abroad over exports from the United States in the
decision of how to supply European and third country
markets was dissipated in the 1970s. The original
stimulus to production and trade from the formation
of the EEC (and the consequent distortions of resource
allocation) had about run its course and enlargement
was being implemented under difficult conditions of
stable or contracting markets and widely divergent
rates of inflation. Since it was the high income
countries of Europe which formed the original EEC,
membership increments in encompassing less affluent
countries will yield less and less economic stimulus
to the bloc. The Tokyo round of GATT tariff negotia-

tions will erode somewhat the degree of trade discrimination in the EEC against the United States and thus make exports an increasingly acceptable alternative to direct foreign investment. The reduced value of the dollar in terms of European currencies gives U.S. exports a new competitive edge in Europe. (This, however, will be a transitory advantage if more rapid U.S. inflation continues and is not corrected by further dollar depreciation.)

Most LDC trading blocs have been too limited in their applicability to have been effective in bringing about any significant expansion of their production or intra-bloc trade. As a consequence, the creation of the bloc did little or nothing to generate new investment there. The Central American Common Market is an exception. Many U.S. manufacturing multinationals established subsidiaries in CACM (largely assembling or packaging operations) during the 1960s. Intra-bloc trade rose from less than 10 percent of the total to over 25 percent before a 1969 political dispute caused two of its members to cease trading with each other. Since then, the share of intra-bloc trade in the total has fallen to about 22 percent and foreign direct investment has declined somewhat, especially in real terms. It seems likely, however, that the establishment of CACM has been an important factor in the volume of U.S. direct investment in the CACM member countries (Annex VII, Table A-III).

Data for ASEAN and LAFTA give an appearance of success to these trading blocs which is misleading. To a large degree intra-member trade was taking place before the formation of the bloc and has continued since, its growth being traceable to the rapid development of member economies rather than to the limited number of tariff concessions in force. (In the case of ASEAN, tariff concessions have only just begun.) Thus, Singapore, because of its position and historic role as an entrepot, always has been a source of imports for its neighbors. Indeed Singapore accounts for over 80 percent of the manufactured goods exchanged among ASEAN members. Brazil, Venezuela, and Mexico, in different ways have also traded fairly extensively with their neighbors. What is important is that especially since the late 1960s, these have been vibrant, dynamic economies, growing rapidly with a strong orientation toward exports. Their exports to their neighbors would have grown even without the trading bloc and they would have attracted foreign capital had they not been bloc members. The existence of LAFTA, however, may have had a marginal role in attracting foreign and U.S. direct investment in manufacturing.

Foreign investment in all of these rapidly growing developing countries has been rising, with Japan and the United States providing the two leading ·sources. At the end of 1976, Indonesia and Brazil were the two top recipients of Japanese private foreign investment. In the ASEAN group, Japan's private investment is larger than that of the U.S. and also more diversified. U.S. direct investment (aggregate to date) in ASEAN is about one-half that of Japan. The Philippines, because of historic ties, seems to have attracted most U.S. manufacturing investment although in recent years Singapore has grown in importance.

LAFTA, however, is the trading bloc which has attracted most U.S. direct manufacturing investment interest outside of Europe (Table A-III, Annex VII). LAFTA as a site for U.S. direct investment in manufacturing has declined in importance over the past 2 decades. In 1960, 15 percent of U.S. manufacturing direct investment went to LAFTA; by 1973 the share was 6 percent. Since then, however, it has recovered, reaching 11 percent in 1976. For the total postwar period (1950-1976), U.S. investment flowing to manufacturing in LAFTA amounted to $8.7 billion, of which 46 percent went to Brazil, 24 percent to Mexico. Argentina was a distant third at 11 percent and in recent years, activity in Venezuela has quickened. These countries are among the most advanced of the LDCs, are rich in natural resources and have established an extensive infrastructure to provide power, transport, and communications. They have also been politically stable countries. In general, most of this investment would have occurred without the tariff concessions brought about by LAFTA which are of too limited application to have played more than a marginal role in investment decisions.

For the other LDC trading blocs, there is no information on direct investment in manufacturing. Investment interest has largely been centered on the extractive industries (uranium in Gabon and Niger, for example, or oil in the Ivory Coast). Such manufacturing investment as has occurred has been in a packaging or assembling operation, attracted by the growing local market rather than the country's membership in a trading bloc.

In summary, where trading blocs have been ineffective in raising the level of production and trade, they have had no significant impact on U.S. direct investment. Where they have been effective in influencing production and trade within the bloc -- as in the EEC during the 1960s and early 1970s and to a much more limited degree EFTA and CACM -- the

depressing effect on U.S. exports of trade diversion
has been compensated at least in part by U.S. direct
investment inside the trading bloc and the provision
to the U.S. subsidiary of U.S. machinery, equipment,
parts, components, materials, and such. During the
1960s, these trends in Europe were exaggerated by
unrealistic exchange rates.

During the second half of the 1970s, investment,
domestic as well as foreign,* has declined worldwide,
economic growth has been stagnant, and world trade
volatile. The EEC is no longer the dynamic force in
the world economy that it was in the previous decade.
The economic future of the world is shifting toward
the advanced developing countries which are growing
rapidly, not because they are members of effective
trading blocs, but because they have been successful
in producing exports for markets in the high income
industrial countries.

---

* In considering Tables II-V, one should recall that
the post-1973 price inflation has born heavily on
machinery and equipment. In addition, exchange rate
fluctuations since 1973 have affected the dollar value
of the reinvested earnings component of direct investment.

3
Licensing Agreements

Introduction

The description of licensing agreements as a middle ground between direct foreign investment and exporting appears to be a valid generalization, although the causes and consequences have varied enormously among individual cases. Since World War II, foreign licensing agreements have gone beyond the simple contract extending to the licensee the legal right to use a patent, trademark, or other industrial property that had prevailed in the prewar years. Agreements have increasingly taken the form of comprehensive contractual arrangements involving the licensor in active participation in ownership and management and providing for furnishing of know-how (processes, design, blueprints, etc.), technical and managerial services and training of foreign managerial and skilled personnel. In part, at least this increase in the coverage of licensing agreements appears to be a response to the increasing complexity of industrial processes, new means of communication, cheaper transportation, and generally more open world markets.

Various advantages and disadvantages to the licensor have been cited. Among the more important advantages are:

1. The possessor of production knowledge or patent rights may derive foreign earnings therefrom without additional capital requirements.

2. A license does not involve major managerial responsibilities.

3. A license granted to a company already well established in the licensed market may enable the

licensor to benefit from sales much larger than he could expect to develop himself -- at least during the effective life of the controlling patent.

4. The licensee may be too strong for the licensor to compete against; a license would be better than a losing fight.

5. A licensor may gain valuable technology through reciprocity.

6. A license may be a stepping stone to direct investment that may or may not involve the same local participants.

7. An overseas market may be separated by tariff barriers into national segments, each of which is too small to justify an American company establishing a subsidiary in it; the separate markets are better reached by separate license.

8. A license may be a means of avoiding exchange controls or reducing taxes.

9. A license may preempt the establishment of a competing local industry.

Among the major disadvantages, the following have been cited:

1. A license may be a means of building up a future competitor -- in the licensee's domestic market, in third countries, perhaps even in the United States.

2. A license typically yields income for a shorter period than does investment.

3. The royalty return may be less than the prospective return on capital.

4. The licensor is dependent upon a management which he does not control. Only indirectly can the licensor influence manufacturing costs, sales, and quality, and, if the product is sold under the licensor's trademark, his reputation may be damaged.

Apparent Postwar Shifts in the Use of Licensing

At the end of the 1950s, it was estimated that the number of U.S. companies that had granted licenses abroad far exceeded the number participating

financially in foreign subsidaries in a ratio of at
least five to one.* This ratio appears to have
diminished since 1960 as the number of new licensing
agreements apparently declined** while the ratio of
fees and royalties received by U.S. corporations
from affiliated enterprises abroad to receipts from
unaffiliated enterprises rose from roughly two-to
one to four-to-one between 1960 and 1977. (Tables
A-IV and A-V) The data thus suggest a shift in the
practice of American industry away from primary
reliance on licensing as a mechanism of foreign
market penetration in favor of licensing in association with direct investment.

This decline in new licensing activity has been
accentuated by growing pressures in the LDCs since
the early 1960s for local participation in business
enterprise located within their boundaries. In
addition, the decline in the number of new licensing
agreements may be somewhat misleading. This would
be true even assuming that the coverage of the sample
on which it is based remained the same throughout its
13-year life (which fact cannot be ascertained and is
doubtful), because of the widespread practice of
renewal of existing agreements and/or shifting to
direct investment from licensing. A 1968 survey of
U.S. licensors in West Germany showed that two-thirds
planned either to renew existing agreements or to
shift to direct investment on the expiration of
current contracts. The continuous increase in fees
and royalties from 1960 through 1977 supports the
deduction that the German practice is widespread.
Licensing is frequently the first step toward direct
investment abroad. The continuous increase in
receipts of fees and royalties from unaffiliated
foreign enterprise further suggests both the renewal
of old licensing agreements and a possible shift
toward increasing participation of larger scale
business over the time period covered. (The royalty
data, however, also reflect price inflation over time
and exchange rate fluctuations.) The increase of
research and development activity in Europe and Japan,
on the other hand, may be responsible for less interest there in U.S. technology and therefore a decline
in the volume of licenses.

---

* Paul R. Potter, "Operating in the Common Market",
Management Review, May 1959.

** See Technical Note to Chapter III for discussion
of data weaknesses.

Worldwide licensing activity appears to have been highly concentrated in manufacturing industries. Of the total number of new agreements negotiated between 1961 and 1973 (the period for which sample data are available), about 90 percent appears to have been in manufacturing; about 1 percent in agriculture, mining, and/or construction. The remainder was in the service industries of which about one-half was in transportation and business services, and one-quarter each in trade (wholesale and retail) and finance.

Small business looms large in the number of new licensing agreements (although this fact may reflect a sample bias giving undue weight to small companies). For the period for which sample data are available, one-half of the licenses were accounted for by licensors whose sales volume was less than $50 million. Licensors with sales of over $500 million accounted for only 20 percent of the number of agreements but probably for the preponderant part of the fees and royalties shown in Table A-IV.

Europe (EEC and EFTA) attracted nearly 40 percent of the new licensing agreements in manufacturing, 1961-1973; about one-fifth were with enterprises in the western hemisphere; over one-fifth in Japan; the remainder in Africa, Asia, and Oceania. Regretably there is no way of knowing whether the relative importance of small business is the same in different regions or concentrated in one region.

Where licensing activity occurred in connection with an affiliated foreign enterprise, the wholly-owned subsidiary was apparently more popular than a foreign branch or a joint venture. In the sample study for the 13-year period, more than half of the new affiliates abroad were wholly-owned subsidiaries; about 10 percent were foreign branches, the remainder, joint ventures. These aggregates reflect the preponderance of licensing activity in the industrial countries (primarily Europe). There two-thirds of the new affiliates were wholly-owned, one-third representing shared ownership. In contrast, in the early 1970s just over half of the affiliates in the developing countries were joint ventures, under one-half wholly-owned. The trend toward unaffiliated enterprise in licensing activity in the developing countries also appears in the data on royalty receipts. In Latin America, for example, the ratio of royalty receipts from affiliated enterprise to receipts from unaffiliated sources declined from about seven-to-one in the late 1960s to five-to-one in the late 1970s. Since in 1956 unaffiliated foreign companies accounted for only 11 percent of royalty receipts from Latin

America, there appears to have been a complete reversal between then and the late 1960s (Table A-IV). Such a trend is not surprising in view of the increasing pressures for local participation in business enterprise in the Third World over the past decade or two.

There is no way of determining to what degree direct investment incorporates licensing activity. The series clearly are related although whether regularly or not is uncertain. The increase since the mid-1960s in the relative and absolute importance of reinvested earning in direct investment totals (and the declining importance of capital outflows) probably reflects the declining stimulus to direct investment and licensing from the earlier formation of the EEC. In the early 1950s reinvested earnings accounted for about two-thirds of total direct investment. The share declined to about 40 percent in the early 1960s. Since then the share has recovered and now represents about three-quarters of the total reinvested earnings. On the other hand, the aggregate impact of FASB-8, the controversial new accounting rules governing the financial reporting in dollars of foreign business activities has probably acted to depress new direct foreign investment; it has certainly added confusion to data interpretation.

In short, the data relating to licensing operations abroad are too incomplete and ambiguous in their relevance to support anything more than highly qualified judgments about what American business has been doing in the aggregate, why it has been behaving in this fashion, or what the consequences of this behavior might be.

LICENSING DATA: SOURCES AND INADEQUACIES

1. Early Department of Commerce Statistics (1956-1957)

Early statistics on receipts of licensing fees
from abroad were first published in the Foreign
Commerce Weekly (December 29, 1958). Coverage included
payments for not only technical rights but proprietary
rights of all kinds, i.e., copyrights and reproduction
rights on books, records, and music. While franchising
agreements were covered, respondents were asked not to
report unless the agreement provided for compensation
over and above the value of materials or supplies
exported from the U.S.

For the years 1956-1957, data on net receipts by
U.S. companies of licensing fees and royalties from
affiliated foreign sources were derived from the returns
of the regular quarterly questionnaire on direct investment activities distributed by the Office of Business
Economics. Affiliated foreign sources were defined as
enterprises in which the licensor owned 25 percent or
more of the equity. Similar receipts from unaffiliated
foreign concerns were estimated from the results of a
special survey. Approximately 1,600 firms were contac-
ted as part of the survey; roughly 650 reported receipts
from such agreements, 750 replied that the questionnaire was not applicable, and from 200 no response
was indicated. Of this final group, most were manu-
facturers of products falling into groups that other
respondents had indicated were not subject to licensing
to any degree.

The sample data appear not to have been inflated
in order to estimate total licensing receipts (in contrast to the years after 1966). They would therefore
be partial but the degree of coverage unknown.

2. U.S. Department of Commerce Balance
    of Payment Activities

    Fees and royalties are defined as:

    "Net receipts by a U.S. reporter from its foreign
    affiliates for professional, administrative, and
    management services and for use of tangible and
    intangible property or rights (patents, tech-
    niques, trademarks, copyrights, etc.)."

    "These figures are net of any fees and royalties
    paid by a U.S. reported to its foreign affiliates
    and also are net of any foreign withholding taxes.
    Receipts of fees and royalties from a foreign
    affiliate by U.S. residents other than the U.S.
    reporter of that foreign affiliate are not in-
    cluded in direct investment fees and royalties."

    Two balance of payment accounts contain data on
receipts of fees and royalties by U.S. firms from
foreign sources. The first is receipt of royalties,
fees, rentals, and service charges from affiliated
corporate sources; the second is receipts for the
same items from unaffiliated sources. Foreign enterprise is listed as affiliated if the licensor owns
10 percent or more of its equity; all other foreign
enterprise is unaffiliated. (Before 1966, however,
the dividing line was 25 percent equity ownership.)
The amount of rentals included is small and appears
to be a payment for the use of machinery when such
is involved in the licensing agreement.
    Both the affiliated and unaffiliated accounts
reflect cumulative totals and not year-of-origin
statistics. Because payments arising from a single
licensing agreement typically continue for a number
of years (an average of 10 years), the receipts of
royalty and licensing fees in any one year reflect
not only agreements newly initiated in that year, but
also compensation paid for technology transferred in
early years.
    Licensing receipts from affiliates do not include
receipts paid by foreigners to foreign branches and
subsidiaries that engage in licensing on behalf of
an American parent. Receipts from such affiliates
would be remitted in the form of profits or dividends.
    The accounts now reflect the response to standard
Department of Commerce questionnaires directed to
approximately 4,000 corporations for receipts from
affiliated sources, and to 650 U.S. concerns for
receipts from unaffiliated sources. The data derived

from this sample are extrapolated to reflect complete
coverage of all fees and royalties on the basis of
returns from a universal survey undertaken in 1966.
A new universal survey for the benchmark year 1977 is
currently being processed and will yield a new, up-
dated basis for extrapolation in the near future.

3.   The Booz·Allen & Hamilton Survey of New
      Foreign Activity of U.S. Firms

      Between 1960 and 1973, Booz·Allen & Hamilton,
Inc. (management consultants) conducted studies of new
foreign business activity of U.S. firms. Three types
of activity were reviewed: new establishments defined
as new business units initiated or acquired, wholly or
partially; the expansion of previously established
business units; and licensing agreements or contract
agreements concluded, involving an exchange of proprietary rights with a foreign group. The data were
compiled from the reports and announcements published
in all major business and financial publications, trade
and consumer magazines, annual reports, and other
documents. All announcements were subsequently cross-
checked against other independent public sources.
      The series was designed to measure the number of
new activities only and complemented other data such
as those produced by the U.S. Department of Commerce
which reports the value in dollars of foreign direct
investment activities. Booz·Allen & Hamilton data
measure the number of new activities only and do not
reflect the magnitude of the dollar amounts involved.
While it was acknowledged that the findings were
generally conservative in that some new foreign
business activity would not be publicly   acknowledged
each year, those responsible for the study emphasized
that most foreign activity represents a significant
corporate decision and therefore a high percentage of
these actions would be made public.
      Using library resources abailable in the Washing-
ton area, Booz·Allen was able to cull area and country licensing data on an annual basis for the fiscal
year 1961-1965 and the calendar years 1969-1973.
The firm released this study in brochure form every
six months through 1968. The results for 1969 and
1970 were published in Business Abroad with all
subsequent reports appearing in the Columbia Journal
of World Business.
      The data are difficult to evaluate and should be
used with caution. Degree of coverage in any one year
is unknown and may vary significantly from year to
year. Thus the reported change in the number of

licensing agreements from one year to the next may
represent a change in coverage rather than a change
in actual licensing activity. For example: Japanese
data from Gaisni Donyu Nenkan: 1968-1969 (Yearbook
on Foreign Capital Entry) show that 388 new licensing
contracts originating in the United States were signed
in 1967 alone while the Booz·Allen survey reports only
139 new U.S. licensing agreements on a worldwide
basis for that same year. The Booz-Allen data are
presented here because they are a unique attempt to
measure new licensing activity. The long-term trends
revealed have more significance than year-to-year
changes and the world totals more reliability than
countries or regions.

4
Varied Effectiveness of Trading Blocs—Past and Future

Causes of Success or Failure

Previous chapters have stressed the limited effectiveness of postwar trading blocs, despite the proliferation of their number. The only truly effective bloc has been the EEC; EFTA would not have been created except for the EEC. The EEC, however, is large enough in relation to world trade to be responsible for the dramatic rise in the share of preferential trade in the total, or the decline in the role of MFN treatment as the basis for world trade. Why have the other blocs not been effective?

The secret of EEC success lies primarily in two factors. The first is the balance of advantage contained in the original agreement (Treaty of Rome) for Germany and France, the two largest members. The free trade area would primarily benefit Germany (the most industrialized member), while the Common Agricultural Policy (CAP), the basis for a common market in agriculture, would most benefit French farmers (the agricultural vote was and remains important in France). The small European member countries expected to benefit from open industrial markets in their larger neighbors, as did northern Italy; southern Italy would benefit from the CAP. Thus there was something for everyone.

Second and equally important, the negotiators of the EEC were national leaders who were in addition statesmen with the vision to appreciate the potential of the common market scheme and the ability to work vigorously, eloquently, and effectively to bring it into being. They laid out a realistic timetable for accomplishing the necessary duty reductions and, supported by firm majorities in their parliaments, were able to reach their goals 2 years ahead of schedule. The political stability of the EEC and EFTA members during the 1960s was of decisive

importance in the success of these blocs, a fact under-
lined by the contrast with LDC trading blocs' lack of
success.
    For the most part the LDCs appear to have lacked
leaders with the same vision, for in the agreements
establishing trading blocs, they have not been able
to negotiate the same kind of balance of advantages
which Europe accomplished. To say that the basic
fault of the LDC trading blocs lies in lack of
complementariness of the economies of their members
(as a number of observers do) misses the point that
most of the LDC blocs have been designed to be
instruments of development. They have included provisions (or at least goals) for an investment program
that would permit the establishment of some degree
of complementariness among members in new industries
to be set up. Their leaders, however, have all too
frequently not been able to agree on where these new
industries would be based or how they would be
financed.
    The problems of negotiation are magnified when
the potential trading bloc contains members at widely
differing stages of development. The more intense
competition that follows the reduction in trade
barriers attendant on the opening of a free trade
area favors the competitor from the more advanced
economy because that firm has been producing for a
larger effective market (higher per capita incomes),
probably for a longer period of time and has the
advantage of both experience and scale over the
competitor from the less developed economy. LAFTA,
for example, recognized this problem and in the early
1960s made provisions to give the less developed member countries special benefits. Despite preferential
treatment for the least developed members in trade and
financial assistance, however, the weaker members felt
it necessary in 1969 to establish their own subbloc
the Andean Common Market. Its progress has been slow,
hampered by conflicting economic philosophies among
member countries and more recently by world recession.
    The Andean subregional group was based on the
belief that economic integration among the least
developed members of a region would serve to prepare
them for eventual transition to membership in the
larger group containing more advanced economies.
This is, of course, the application on a lower level
of aggregation of the basic concept motivating all
LDC trading blocs - that a free trade area together
with a program for regional integration will provide
a mechanism for economic development. The creation
of subgroups within a trading bloc was conceived as

an instrument for overcoming the difficulties of
implementation introduced by differing levels of
development and thus as a crutch for leaders who were
not able to reach agreement among themselves. The
validity of the basic idea is not denied by the failure
of its implementation. Indeed the success of CACM
during its first decade in confirmation that the basic
thesis will work - politics permitting. (See Annex IV)

Although ASEAN as a trading bloc is too recent
to have been adequately tested, ASEAN as an instrument
of economic and political cooperation has experienced
a degree of success that has surprised most observers.
ASEAN successes, in fact, began in 1976 with the U.S.
disengagement in Vietnam. It would appear that the
withdrawal of the United States from the region so
concentrated the minds of the leaders of ASEAN's
members that they were able to suppress long-standing
antagonisms when confronted by a potentially hostile
regional climate. This mental concentration has
probably recently been buttressed by Vietnam's
incursion into Cambodia and China's response. If so,
ASEAN as a trading bloc might be more successful than
the average non-European bloc; its leaders have shown
more evidence of statesmanship.

Trading blocs have been part of the African scene
for many years; the predecessors of some of today's
organizations are to be found in the nineteenth century
colonial era. Today's blocs, however, suffer all of
the ills which beset other LDC efforts: political
instability; national jealousies and antagonisms;
weak leaders; diverse degrees of development and
economic strength; lack of infrastructure appropriate
to intra-regional as opposed to overseas trade. Annex
V contains a precis of the experience of African
trading blocs.

The Outlook

Our previous discussion has indicated that trading
blocs are not immune from the forces affecting the
volume of world trade. The success of the EEC during
the 1960s drew on and contributed to the general postwar expansion of economic activity that was in train
when the EEC was born. The climate at that time was
congenial to EEC success. Markets were expanding,
exchange rates were favorable, capital and labor were
available in increasing amounts and raw materials
existed in relative plenty. The fact that all member
countries were led by coalition governments of parties
of the political center is worth stressing; in addition
parliamentary majorities were strong. This meant that

member governments were generally of the same political
philosophy, which facilitated agreement, and had sufficient domestic political strength to permit them to
make concessions where necessary.
    The future does not hold the promise of such a
favorable climate for European growth. The earlier
discussion has indicated that the stimulus to growth
from tariff reduction and its associated investment
surge has about run its course. The impetus to
European expansion from this source will continue to
diminish in the years ahead. By itself, this will
act to retard the rate growth of world trade.
    In addition, the financial and structural
imbalances in the world economy (and especially among
the industrial countries) will serve further to retard
the growth of world trade. The size of U.S. payments
deficit is forcing this country to abandon its attempt
to achieve a payments balance by raising its exports
to the level of imports and is forcing it to curtail
domestic expansion and risk negative growth in order
to curtail imports as well as inflation. Balance is
likely to be achieved at least as much from import
retardation as from export growth.
    The existing industrial structures of the United
States, Europe, and to a smaller degree Japan, have
been made obsolete by the high level of energy prices
and by the increasing size of certain export industries in the developing countries. Steel, chemicals,
shipbuilding,. consumer electronics have varying
degrees of overcapacity in the industrial countries
and must be contracted if world trade in these products
is to recover or be maintained at its current levels.
Shifting resources out of declining industries into
growth industries becomes vastly more difficult if
markets in the aggregate are not bouyant and if the
economy is already plagued with unemployment.
Attempts to protect these import-impacted industries
in the rich countries will curtail growth in the most
rapidly expanding areas of the world. Various efforts
of this sort have already been successful and their
effects are cumulating. The GATT agreements negotiated
in the Tokyo Round contained a "safeguard" provision
spelling out conditions under which such attempts can
legally be made in the future. The safeguard code
was perhaps the most controversial in the entire
Round; its acceptance is still in doubt.
    Further, it seems likely that the rapid expansion
of the oil-exporting economies and therefore of their
imports will slow. The revolution in Iran will act
directly toward this end and is indirectly likely to
serve as a chastening example to the leaders of other

rapidly developing economies, with or without oil exports. In fact, the vivid Iranian example of the hazards of too rapid growth is likely to cause a deliverate stretching out of development programs in all those rapidly developing countries led by auto-cratic leaders. In the case of those countries faced by a clear and immediate external threat, however, (e.g. Korea, Taiwan, and the ASEAN countries) the imminent danger may be sufficient to continue to rally support for the strong leader whose economic policies are perceived as building up the country's capacity to defend itself.

Even the successful conclusion of the Tokyo Round does not assure its successful implementation. The main accomplishment of a successful Round will lie, not in tariff reductions, which are small com-pared to the Kennedy Round, but in the new codes of conduct which aim to reduce non-tariff barriers to trade. Just because non-tariff barriers are less obvious, they are easier to effect and harder to police. Non-compliance with the codes will be diffi-cult to prove; if nations want to circumvent the new rules, it will not be difficult. Because the climate for trade expansion is not likely to be congenial, many nations may in fact undertake to circumvent the new rules should they come into being.

LDC trading blocs found it difficult to get started when world markets were expanding and the general climate for trade and investment was favorable. It seems unlikely that they will make much progress in an era of slow growth and uncertainty stemming from high inflation and structural and financial imbalances.

Despite this gloomy outlook, there are a few potential bright spots on the world scene. Mexico's new bargaining strength, courtesy of its recent oil and natural gas discoveries, is likely to assure its continued access to the U.S. market, (which already absorbs three-fifths of its exports), as well as to Europe and Japan. Mexico is blessed by stable poli-tical institutions; the most important risk to Mexico's future as a locus for foreign investment lies in the potential impact of its mushrooming population on its long-term political stability. For the next 5 years at least, this risk should be small.

Brazil's enormous wealth of natural resources and continental size suggest that it has more capacity for internally oriented growth than most developing countries, given the investment resources. Brazil's recent economic accomplishments have been fueled by an inflow of foreign capital -- equity and credit -- and policies which have succeeded in marshalling

capital from domestic sources to an unprecedented
degree. If the retardation in world economic growth
is moderate, if markets in the industrial countries
remain relatively open and if further increases in
the price of oil do no more than keep pace with world
inflation -- all important qualifications -- Brazil's
above-average growth rate should continue. Although
there is some danger of political instability during
the next 5 years, the risk and the degree of instability are hard to assess at present.

In the second half of the 1970s, ASEAN has
attracted considerable attention as a growth area,
and justifiably so. A recent issue of The Economist
pointed out that if recent ASEAN growth rates continue,
the rich capitalist world will soon be made up of a
"big four": The United States, EEC, Japan, and ASEAN.
At independence, each member country faced its own
set of internal political challenges and each has
coped successfully. Leadership is strong, authori-
tarian, and of uncommonly high quality. Political
stability seems assured. Members welcome foreign
investment and have initiated work on a proposal to
standardize investment procedures among the five to
make it easier for foreign enterprise to enter the
bloc.

The ASEAN leaders themselves place most hope for
their economic future in expanded relations with the
EEC, despite the larger investment roles of Japan and
the United States. This enthusiasm for Europe is a
consequence both of former colonial ties and the EEC
system of preferences that offers more to ASEAN than
that of any other developed country. All members
share an apprehension about becoming too dependent on
Japan. Although the success of ASEAN's recently initiated preferential trading scheme is by no means
assured, the outlook for the continued rapid growth
of member countries is bright.

Thus, assuming that the United States and Europe
do not turn inward and pursue a rigorously protectionist course, Singapore, Thailand, and Malaysia will
make ASEAN an increasing force in world trade. Brazil,
Mexico, and Venezuela are likely to do the same for
LAFTA. And if a new generation of statesmen should
assume the leadership of LAFTA, Latin America could
finally come into its own as a dynamic force in the
world economy.

Selected Bibliography

Booz·Allen & Hamilton, Inc. "Five Years of New
    Foreign Business Activity of U.S. Firms."
    Business Abroad, July 1965.
Bradshaw, Marie T. "U.S. Exports to Foreign Affiliates
    of U.S. Firms" Survey of Current Business, May 1969.
Business Week. "Licensing: Middle Way to Profits
    Abroad," March 22, 1958, p. 109-111.
Casadio, Gian Paolo. "Trade Across the Atlantic: From
    the Kennedy Round to Neo-Protectionism." Lo
    Spettatore Internazionale, No. 1 (1972).
    Instituto Affari Internazionale, Rome.
Collier, Thomas P. "What You Should Know About Pro-
    tecting Your Company Name, Trademark, and Know-how."
    Business Abroad, August 1969.
Congressional Research Service, "Regulations of Direct
    Foreign Investment in Australia, Canada, France,
    Japan, Mexico" Foreign Investment Act of 1975.
    Hearings Before the Subcommittee on Banking,
    Housing & Urban Affairs. U.S. Senate 94th
    Congress 1st Session 1975.
Cutler, Frederick. U.S. Direct Investments Abroad
    1966 - Part I: Balance of Payments Data. U.S.
    Department of Commerce, Washington, D.C. 1970.
Dun's Review. "Does Foreign Licensing Pay?" October
    1969, p. 99-105.
Drummond, Stuart, ASEAN: "The Growth of an Economic
    Dimension." The World Today, January 1979.
Ghai, Yash P. "East African Industrial Licensing
    System: A Device for The Regional Allocation of
    Industry?" Journal of Common Market Studies,
    1968. Vol. XII No. 3. p. 265-295.
Hartland-Thunberg, Penelope. The Political and Strategic
    Importance of Exports. CSIS. Significant Issues
    Series. Vol I No. 3. Washington 1979.
Hymer, S. H. The International Operations of National
    Firms. Cambridge, Mass.: MIT Press 1976. p. 46-64.
International Commerce. "New focus on Licensing Affords
    Chance to Assess its Advantages." April 22, 1968.
    p. 20-21.
Jurecky, John P. "Surveys Report U.S. Firms' View on
    Licensing Agreements, German Readiness to Conclude
    Still More." International Commerce, April 8, 1968.
    p. 20-21.
Lang, Eugene L. "In defense of Licensing..." Business
    Abroad, May 16, 1966. p. 35-36.
Lukens, W. L. "Licensing Your Product for Manufacture
    Abroad..." Business Abroad, April 18, 1966.
    p. 30-31.

46

McDermott, Arthur P. "Licensing is Middle Route." International Commerce, December 23, 1968. p. 6-8.

Musgrave, Peggy B., "Direct Investment Abroad and the Multinationals: Effects on the United States Economy" U.S. Government Printing Office, Washington, D.C., 1975.

National Academy of Sciences. Technology, Trade, and the U.S. Economy. Washington, D.C., 1978.

OECD Occasional Studies. The Measurement of Domestic Cyclical Fluctuations. Paris, July 1973.

Porter, Paul R. "Operating in the Common Market..." The Management Review, May 1959, p. 19-82.

Reuninger, John P. Multinational Cooperation for Development in West Africa. Pergamon Press, NY 1979.

Rhodes, John B. "U.S. New Business Activities Abroad." Columbia Journal of World Business, Summer 1974. p. 19-105.

-----"Upturn in Foreign Activity by U.S. Firms." Columbia Journal of World Business, Summer 1973.

-----"U.S. Investment Abroad: Who's going Where, How and Why." Columbia Journal of World Business, Summer 1972. p. 33-40.

-----"American Investment Abroad: Who's going Where, How and Why." Business Abroad, June 1971. p. 6-9.

-----"Where and How U.S. Companies are Moving and Expanding in Overseas Markets." Business Abroad, May 1970. p. 14-19.

Scheinfeld, Aaron. "Interview with Aaron Scheinfeld." Business Abroad, September 19, 1966.

Shonfield, Andrew. Europe: Journey to an Unknown Destination." Penguin Books, 1973.

-----International Economic Relations of the Western World 1959-1971. Vol I, Politics & Trade. Royal Institute of International Affairs, London 1976.

Smith, J. E. "U.S. Firms Conduct Lively Technical Exchanges with Foreign Companies." Foreign Commerce Weekly, December 29, 1958. pps. 3-4, 15.

Tesar, George. "Dynamics of Export Consulting." Paper presented at National Meeting of the Academy of International Business, NY, November 12-14, 1976.

Travglini, Vincent D. "Licensing, Joint Ventures Aid Technology Transfer." International Commerce, July 28, 1969. p. 2-6.

-----"Licensing U.S. Know-how Abroad is Increasing." International Commerce, July 25, 1966. p. 2-5.

Vernon, Raymond, "Economic Consequences of U.S. Foreign Direct Investment" U.S. National Economic Policy in an Interdependent World (Williams Report) Washington, D.C. Government Printing Office, 1971.

-----"The Multinationals: No Strings Attached." Foreign Policy, Winter 1979.

Annex I
List of Trading Blocs:
Customs Unions and Free Trade Areas, 1978

1. African and Mauritian Common Organization (OCAM):

Senegal	Gabon	Burundi
Mali	Upper Volta	Rwanda
Ivory Coast	Benin	Mauritius
Niger	Congo	
Togo	(Brazzaville)	
Central African Empire	Zaire	

2. Andean Subregional Group (ANCOM):

Colombia	Ecuador	Bolivia
Venezuela	Peru	Chile

3. Association of South-East Asian Nations (ASEAN):

Thailand	Singapore	Philippines
Malaysia	Indonesia	

4. Caribbean Common Market (CARICOM):

Belize	Dominica	Barbados
Jamaica	St. Lucia	Trinidad and
Antigua	St. Vincent	Tobago
Montserrat	Grenada	Guyana

5. Central American Common Market (CACM):

Guatemala	Honduras	Costa Rica
El Salvador	Nicaragua	

6. Council of the Entente States:

Ivory Coast	Togo	Benin
Niger	Upper Volta	

7. East African Common Market (EACM):

Uganda	Kenya	Tanzania

8. European Economic Community (EEC):

Denmark   Ireland   France
United Kingdom   Netherlands   Federal Republic
  and Northern   Belgium and   of Germany
  Ireland   Luxembourg   Italy

Countries with Special Associations with the EEC:

Spain   Greece   Israel
Portugal   Turkey   Morocco
Malta and Gozo   Cyprus   Algeria

9. European Free Trade Association (EFTA):

Iceland   Norway   Switzerland
Sweden   Austria   Portugal

Associate member -
Finland

10. Latin American Free Trade Association (LAFTA):

Mexico   Peru   Paraguay
Colombia   Bolivia   Uruguay
Venezuela   Chile   Argentina
Ecuador   Brazil

11. Maghreb Group:

Morocco   Algeria   Tunisia

12. Union of Central African States (UDEAC):

Cameroon   Gabon   Congo
Central African   (Brazzaville)
  Empire

13. West African Economic Community (CEAO):

Mauritania   Ivory Coast   Upper Volta
Senegal   Niger   Benin
Mali

Source: Tariff Schedules of the United States
         Annotated (1978) Annex B, p. B-16, 17.

Annex II
Vital Statistics of Trading Blocs

1.   Common Afro-Mauritian Organization (OCAM).

Established February 1965.

Afro-Malagasy Union for Economic Cooperation (UAMCE) was founded in December 1960 by 12 former French colonies. At the UAM meeting in March 1963, the UAMCE was established to begin operations in February 1964.

OCAM is the successor to UAMCE.

Current members:

1.	Benin (Dahomey)	2/65 - present
2.	Central African Empire (Republic)	2/65 - present
3.	Ivory Coast	2/65 - present
4.	Niger	2/65 - present
5.	Senegal	2/65 - present
6.	Togo	2/65 - present
7.	Upper Volta	2/65 - present
8.	Rwanda	5/65 - present
9.	Mauritius	70 - present
10.	Seychelles	77 - present

Past members:

11.	Mauritania	2/65 - 6/65, currently participates in technical programs
12.	Gabon	2/65 - 9/76, currently associated
13.	Zaire (Congo-Kinshasa)	5/65 - 73
14.	Congo-Brazzaville	2/65 - 73
15.	Cameroon	2/65 - 74
16.	Chad	2/65 - 74
17.	Madagascar	2/65 - 74

50

Aims:

The objectives proposed in 1965 included customs reform,
possibly leading to the establishment of an African
Common Market, and common economic policies covering
investment, insurance of trade and restrictions on
double taxation. A stabilization fund was projected,
to support commodity prices.

Since the 1974 summit at Bangui, the aims of the
organization have been expressed in a new form.
Instead of an all-African Common Market, the aim is
more practicably to bring the economic communities
of Africa within a single confederation. A solidarity
and guarantee fund has been established to encourage
credit from overseas and give assistance to the
poorest member countries.

At an extraordinary conference in Dakar, Senegal, it
was decided to leave political matters to other bodies
(principally the UN and the OAU) and concentrate on
strengthening African cooperation in economic,
technical, cultural, and social development.

2. Andean Common Market (Commission of the Cartegena
Agreement) (ANCOM).

Established May 1969.

Current members:

1.	Bolivia	5/69 - present
2.	Colombia	5/69 - present
3.	Ecuador	5/69 - present
4.	Peru	5/69 - present
5.	Venezuela	73 - present

Past member:

6.	Chile	5/69 - 10/76

Aims:

Achieve balanced and coordinated development of member
countries by means of economic development of member
countries by means of economic integration; facilitate
members' participation in the process of integration
provided for in the Montevideo Treaty; work to establish favorable conditions for the development of the
LAFTA common market, the over-riding consideration
being a continual rise in the standard of living of
the inhabitants of the region.

3. Association of South-East Asian Nations (ASEAN).

Established August 1967.

Successor to ASA

Members:

1.	Indonesia	8/67 - present
2.	Malaysia	8/67 - present
3.	Philippines	8/67 - present
4.	Singapore	8/67 - present
5.	Thailand	8/67 - present

Aims:

ASEAN was established in 1967 with the signing of the ASEAN Declaration, otherwise known as the Bangkok Declaration. This set out the objectives of the organization as follows:

To accelerate the economic growth, social progress and cultural development in the region through joint endeavours in the spirit of equality and partnership in order to strengthen the foundation for a prosperous and peaceful community of South-East Asian nations.

To promote regional peace and stability through abiding respect for justice and the rule of law in the relationship among countries of the region and adherence to the principles of the United Nations Charter.

To promote active collaboration and mutual assistance on matters of common interest in the economic, social, cultural, technical, scientific, and administrative fields.

To provide assistance to each other in the form of training and research facilities in the educational, professional, technical, and administrative spheres.

To collaborate more effectively for the greater utilization of their agriculture and industries, the expansion of their trade, including the study of the problems of international commodity trade, the improvement of their transportation and communication facilities, and the raising of the living standards of their people.

To promote South-East Asian studies.

To maintain close and beneficial cooperation with existing international and regional organizations with similar aims and purposes, and explore all avenues for even closer cooperation among themselves.

4. Caribbean Common Market (CARICOM).

Established July 1973.

Successor to CARIFTA, established January 1967.

Members:

1.	Barbados	7/73 - present (CARIFTA 12/65-7/73)
2.	Guyana	7/73 - present (CARIFTA 12/65-7/73)
3.	Jamaica	7/73 - present (CARIFTA 6/68-7/73)
4.	Trinidad and Tobago	7/73 - present (CARIFTA 2/68-7/73)
5.	Belize	5/74 - present (CARIFTA 6/70-5/74)
6.	Dominica	5/75 - present
7.	Grenada	5/74 - present
8.	Monserrat	5/74 - present
9.	St. Lucia	5/74 - present
10.	St. Vincent	5/74 - present
11.	Antigua	7/74 - present (CARIFTA 12/65-5/74)
12.	St. Kitts-Nevis-Anguilla	7/74 - present

Aims:

Provide for the establishment of a common external tariff and a common protective policy for trade with outside countries; adopt a scheme for the harmonization of fiscal incentives to industry and of double taxation arrangements; coordinate economic policies and development planning; set up a special regime for the less developed countries of the Community.

5. Central American Common Market (CACM) (ODECA).

Established December 1960.

5. CACM (cont'd).

Members:

1.	Guatemala	12/60 - present
2.	El Salvador	12/60 - present
3.	Nicaragua	12/60 - present
4.	Costa Rica	62 - present
5.	Honduras	12/60 - presently a member, de jure, but withdrew, de facto, in 1969.

Aims:

Promote the integration of the Central American economies and coordinate the economic policies of the Contracting States.

6. Council of the Entente States.

A political and economic association of five states giving priority to economic coordination in member states.

Founded May 1959.

Members:

1.	Benin	5/59 - present
2.	Ivory Coast	5/59 - present
3.	Niger	5/59 - present
4.	Upper Volta	5/59 - present
5.	Togo	6/66 - present

Aims:

Promote economic development in the region; to assist in preparing specific projects and to mobilize funds from other sources; to act as a guarantee fund to encourage investments in the region; to encourage trade and investment between the member states.

Since 1974 it has been empowered to finance the reduction of interest rates and the extension of maturity periods of foreign loans to member countries.

7. <u>East African Common Market (EACM)</u>.

Established June 1967.

Successor to East African Common Services Organization, established December 1961.

Members:

1.	Kenya	6/67 - present
2.	Tanzania	6/67 - present
3.	Uganda	6/67 - present

Aims:

Strengthen and regulate the industrial, commercial,
and other relations between Kenya, Uganda, and
Tanzania in order to bring about accelerated and
balanced development for the benefit of all.

8. <u>European Economic Community (EEC)</u>.

Established January 1958.

Members:

1.	Belgium	1/58 - present
2.	France	1/58 - present
3.	Federal Republic of Germany	1/58 - present
4.	Italy	1/58 - present
5.	Luxembourg	1/58 - present
6.	Netherlands	1/58 - present
7.	United Kingdom	1/73 - present
8.	Ireland	1/73 - present
9.	Denmark	1/73 - present

Associate members:

10. Cyprus
11. Greece
12. Malta
13. Turkey

Applied for membership:

14. Portugal   (3/77)
15. Spain   (6/77)

(In addition, 46 Lomé Convention (see Lomé Convention
page 59) states have negotiated preferential arrangements
with the EEC.)

8. **EEC (cont'd)**.

Aims:

Promote throughout the Community a harmonious development of economic activities, a continuous and balanced
expansion, an increase in mobility, an acceleration in
the rise of the standard of living and closer relations
between its Member States, by establishing a common
market and by progressive rapprochement of the economic
policies of Member States.

9. **European Free Trade Association (EFTA)**.

Established January 1960.

Current members:

1.	Austria	1/60 - present
2.	Norway	1/60 - present
3.	Portugal	1/60 - present
4.	Sweden	1/60 - present
5.	Switzerland	1/60 - present
6.	Iceland	3/70 - present

Associate member:

7.	Finland	61 - present

Former members:

8.	United Kingdom	1/60 - 1/73
9.	Denmark	1/60 - 1/73

Aims:

Promote in the area of the Association and in each
Member State a sustained expansion of economic
activity, full employment, increased productivity and
the rational use of resources, financial stability
and continuous improvement in living standards, secure
that trade between Member States takes place in conditions of fair competition, avoid significant dis-
parity between Member States in the conditions of
supply of raw materials produced within the area of
the Association, and contribute to the harmonious
development and expansion of world trade and to the
progressive removal of barriers to it.

56

10. Latin American Free Trade Association (LAFTA).

Established January 1961.

Members:

1.	Argentina	2/61 - present
2.	Bolivia	67 - present
3.	Brazil	2/61 - present
4.	Chile	2/61 - present
5.	Colombia	10/61 - present
6.	Ecuador	10/61 - present
7.	Mexico	2/61 - present
8.	Paraguay	2/61 - present
9.	Peru	2/61 - present
10.	Uruguay	2/61 - present
11.	Venezuela	9/66 - present

Aims:

Gradually eliminate from the essential part of their reciprocal trade all types of duties and restrictions that affect the importation of goods originating in the territory of any contracting party.

11. Maghreb Group

Maghreb Permanent Consultive Committee.

Established October 1964.

Members:

1.	Algeria	10/64 - present
2.	Morocco	10/64 - present
3.	Tunisia	10/64 - present
4.	Mauritania	75 - present

Past member:

5.	Libya	10/64 - 1970

The Maghreb Committee is a forum for inter-governmental consultation and the exchange of technical information. Its purpose is to investigate all problems relating to economic cooperation in the member countries. At the request of the Conference of Ministers of Economy or as part of the programme agreed by the Ministers, it proposes measures designed to reinforce cooperation and to bring into being a Maghreb Economic Community.

12. Central African Customs and Economics Union (UDEAC).

Established December 1964, in force January 1966.

Successor to Equatorial Customs Union (UDE), established 1959.

Current members:

1.	Cameroon	12/64 - present (UDE 6/61-12/64)
2.	Congo-Brazzaville	12/64 - present (UDE 59-12/64)
3.	Gabon	12/64 - present (UDE 59-12/64)
4.	Central African Empire (Republic)	12/64 - 4/68 and 12/68 - present (UDE 59-12/64) (UEAC 4/68-12/68)

Past member:

5.	Chad	12/64 - 4/68, observer status 4/75 - present. (Joined UDEAC 4/68 with Central African Republic and Zaire.)

Aims:

Customs union: trade between the member countries is duty free. A common external tariff applies to imports from third countries; this is the principal import tariff, to which the member governments may if necessary add supplementary duties.

13. West African Economic Community (CEAO).

Established 1959 as UDEAO (Customs Union of West African Countries), reorganized May 1970 as CEAO.

Members:

1.	Ivory Coast	1959 - present
2.	Mali	1959 - present
3.	Mauritania	1959 - present
4.	Niger	1959 - present
5.	Senegal	1959 - present
6.	Upper Volta	1959 - present

58

13. CEAO (cont'd).

Observer status:

    7. Benin (Dahomey)   member 1959-1973,
                                observer 1974-present
    8. Togo

Aims:

The West African Economic Community will go beyond the
West African Customs Union in coordinating not only
customs and trade measures but also the development
of policies with regard to transport and communica-
tions, cattle and beef, industry, external trade,
tourism, energy, research, etc.

It will develop trade between member states in
agricultural and industrial products, through the
establishment of an area of organized trade; and it
will develop regional economic cooperation policies,
in particular as regards industry and transport.

Sources: Handbook of International Organizations;
           Statesman's Year Book; EUROPA.

THE LOMÉ CONVENTION

(Addendum to European Economic Community)

Concluded at Lomé, Togo, in February 1975 by the European Community and 46 African, Caribbean and Pacific (ACP) states, the Convention now applies to 52 developing countries.

The European Community

Belgium	Ireland	United Kingdom
Denmark	Italy	
France	Luxembourg	
Federal Republic of Germany	Netherlands	

The ACP States

Bahamas	Guyana	Surinam
Barbados	Ivory Coast	Swaziland
Benin	Jamaica	Tanzania
Botswana	Kenya	Togo
Burundi	Lesotho	Tonga
Cameroon	Liberia	Trinidad and Tobago
Cape Verde	Madagascar	
Central African Empire	Malawi	Upper Volta
	Mali	Western Samoa
Chad	Mauritania	Zaire
Comoros	Mauritius	Zambia
Congo	Niger	
Equatorial Guinea	Nigeria	
	Papua New Guinea	
Ethiopia	Rwanda	
Fiji	Sao Tomé and Principe	
Gabon		
Gambia	Senegal	
Ghana	Seychelles	
Guinea	Sierra Leone	
Guinea-Bissau	Somalia	
Grenada	Sudan	

Functions

The Convention, which came into force on April 1, 1976, replaces the Yaoundé Conventions and the Arusha Agreement, providing a new framework of cooperation and taking into account the states newly associated with the Community through the accession of the United Kingdom. It has also been extended to apply to countries which were not former dependencies of Community member states. The European Council agreed in March 1977 to consider a further extension, applying some elements of the Convention to developing countries in other world regions.

Annex III
Indicators of Market Size:
Tables III-1 – III-42

Explanatory Notes

Where a column is blank, the amount involved in
negligible and/or unreported.

The statistical reporting systems of least
developed countries are rudimentary and sometimes
quixotic. Large segments of the population are
frequently outside the bounds of the market economy
and excluded from statistical coverage; definitions
of "manufacturing" often include handicrafts. Reliability is questionable, although it does tend to
improve through time as coverage is extended and
techniques strengthened. The fact of improved
coverage through time, however, means that growth
rates are overstated.

GNP data in dollars have been converted at
average 1976 exchange rates.

Source: United Nations: U.S. Bureau of Mines; World
           Almanac.

Table III-1

INDICATORS OF MARKET SIZE:

AFRICAN AND MAURITIAN COMMON ORGANIZATION (OCAM)

	Total GNP at market prices 1976 (US $ in millions)	GNP per capita at market prices 1976 (US $)	Average Annual GNP per capita growth rate 1960-1976	Population mid-1976 (000)	Average Annual population growth rate 1970-1976
Benin	570	180	0.0	3,200	1.5
Burundi	470	120	2.2	3,860	2.3
Central African Empire	430	240 1/	0.3 1/	1,827	2.2
Congo	730	530	1.3	1,360	2.3
Gabon	2,050	3,780	6.7	544	1.7
Ivory Coast	4,560	650	3.3	7,025	4.3
Mali	600	100	0.9	5,840	2.5
Mauritius	610	680	1.3	894	1.3
Niger	700	150	-1.6	4,730	2.8
Rwanda	510	120	0.8	4,217	2.3
Senegal	2,110	410	-0.4	5,135	2.7
Togo	620	270	4.1	2,280	2.6
Upper Volta	640	100	0.6	6,170	2.3
Zaire	3,190	130	1.4	25,389	2.7
TOTALS	17,790	245		72,471	

Note:
1/ Tentative

Table III-2

INDICATORS OF MARKET SIZE:
AFRICAN AND MAURITIAN COMMON ORGANIZATION (OCAM)

	GDP in local currency	GDP in Manufacturing	%	GDP in Construction	%	GDP in Agriculture	%
Benin	148.5 100 million CFA francs	10.1 1/ (1977)	6%	4.9	3%	56.5	38%
Burundi	340						
Central African Empire	US $ million (1974) 57.1	5.4 (1974)	9%	1.8	3%	18.4	32%
Congo	1000 million CFA francs (1971) 500						
Gabon	US $ million (1974) 462.4	23.0 (1975)	4%	79.8	17%	40.8	8%
Ivory Coast	1000 million CFA francs (1975) 1,582.5	183.3 (1977)	11	114.2	7%	369.9	23%
Mali	1000 million CFA francs (1977) .32						
Mauritius	US $ million (1971) 4,423 million rupees (1976)	914	20%	331	7%	811	18%
Niger	97,808 million CFA francs (1969)	6,282	6%	3,144	3%	50,101	51%
Rwanda	28.7 1000 million R. francs (1974)	1.3	4%	0.9	3%	17.0	59%

Table III-2 (cont'd)

	GDP in local currency	GDP in Manufacturing	%	GDP in Construction	%	GDP in Agriculture	%
Senegal	1.57 US $ billion (1975)						
Togo	86,716 million CFA francs (1972)	7,448	8%	4,034	4%	29,560	34%
Upper Volta	109.6 1000 million CFA francs (1974)	11.3	10%	5.3	4%	45.1	41%
Zaire	1,847.4 million zaires (1975)	199.6	10%	103.2	5%	350.7	18%

Note:
1/ Includes mining

Table III-3

INDICATORS OF MARKET SIZE:

AFRICAN AND MAURITIAN COMMON ORGANIZATION (OCAM)

	Employees in Manufacturing (%)	Crude steel production (1000 metric tons) Monthly Avgs.	Coal production (1000 metric tons) Monthly Avgs.	Electricity Generated millions of KWH Monthly Avgs.	Railways Freight ton/KLM Monthly
Benin	(1970) 12%			(1975) 4.75	(1977) 11.6
Burundi				(1976) 2.27	none
Central African Empire				(1975) 4.33	none
Congo	(1972) 2% [1]			(1977) 10	(1977) 42.4
Gabon	(1964) 1%			(1976) 19 [2]	(1977) 45.9 [3]
Ivory Coast	(1970) 4%			(1977) 100 [2]	(1977) 12.4
Mali				(1975) 5.8	
Mauritius				(1977) 32 [4]	
Niger	(1970) 2%			(1975) 5.8	none
Rwanda	(1968) 13%			(1975) 11.7	none
Senegal	(1970) 6%			(1976) 38 [2]	(1976) 13.7
Togo				(1976) 6.3	(1976) 3.14 [5]
Upper Volta				(1975) 4.38	(1975) 37
Zaire	(1970) 11%		(1977) 10	(1977) 126	(1973) 251.4
TOTAL				370	

Notes:
1/ Includes commerce and industry
2/ Production by industry negligible
3/ Includes service traffic
4/ Includes generation by industry establishment primarily for their own use
5/ Includes passenger baggage, parcel post

Table III-4

INDICATORS OF MARKET SIZE:

ANDEAN SUBREGIONAL GROUP (ANCOM)

	Total GNP at market prices 1976 (US $ in millions)	GNP per capita at market prices 1976 (US $)	Average Annual GNP per capita growth rate 1960-1976	Population mid-1976 (000)	Average Annual population growth rate 1970-1976
Bolivia	2,970	510	2.3	5,794	2.7
Chile	10,870	1,050	1.1	10,375	1.8
Colombia	15,740	650	2.7	24,301	2.8
Ecuador	5,100	700	3.0 1/	7,306	3.5
Peru	13,450	840	2.5	16,068	3.0
Venezuela	31,340	2,540	2.6	12,361	3.1
TOTALS	79,470	1,043		76,205	

Note:
1/ 1965-1976

Table VII-5
INDICATORS OF MARKET SIZE:

ANDEAN SUBREGIONAL GROUP (ANCOM)

	GDP in local currency	GDP in Manufacturing	%	GDP in Construction	%	GDP in Agriculture	%
Bolivia	50,156 million pesos (1975)	6,603	13%	2,154	4%	9,022	18%
Chile	321,188 million pesos (1977)	65,468	20%	6,315	2%	33,011	10%
Colombia	419,013 million pesos (1975)	91,927	22%	20,165	5%	114,180	27%
Ecuador	153,812 million sucres (1977)	25,748	17%	9,671	6%	31,279	20%
Peru	827.7 1000 million soles (1976)	235.5	28%	33.2	4%	105.6	13%
Venezuela	152,796 million bolivares (1977)	24,972	16%	10,689	7%	9,527	6%

Table III-6
INDICATORS OF MARKET SIZE:
ANDEAN SUBREGIONAL GROUP (ANCOM)

	Index number manufacturing employment 1970 = 100	Crude steel production (1000 metric tons) Monthly Avgs.	Coal production (1000 metric tons) Monthly Avgs.	Electricity Generated millions of KWH Monthly Avgs.	Railways Freight ton/KLM Monthly Avgs.
Bolivia				(1975) 83.3	(1973) 195 1/
Chile	(1977) 93.9	(1977) 42 2/	(1977) 103	(1977) 82.2	(1977) 184
Colombia	(1977) 122.3	(1977) 18	(1976) 3,620	(1977) 1,118	(1977) 101.3 4/
Ecuador	(1975) 120.7			(1975) 107.5	(1975) 3.85
Peru	(1972) 131 1/	(1976) 349 3/	(1973) 10	(1977) 275	(1976) 63
Venezuela	(1977) 139.8	(1977) 68	(1977) 10.1	(1976) 1,939.7	(1971) .77 5/
TOTALS				4,345.5	

Notes:
1/ Percent employees in manufacturing
2/ Ingots only
3/ For casting only
4/ Including service traffic
5/ Million net ton-miles

Table III-7

INDICATORS OF MARKET SIZE:

ASSOCIATION OF SOUTH-EAST ASIAN NATIONS (ASEAN)

	Total GNP at market prices 1976 (US $ in millions)	GNP per capita at market prices 1976 (US $)	Average Annual GNP per capita growth rate 1960-1976	Population mid-1976 (000)	Average Annual population growth rate 1970-1976
Indonesia	36,120	280	3.1	130,887	1.8
Malaysia	10,560	830	3.9	12,653	2.7
Philippines	17,990	420	2.4	43,293	2.7
Singapore	5,870	2,580 1/	7.5	2,278	1.6
Thailand	16,300	380	4.6	42,960	2.8
TOTALS	86,840			232,071	

Note:
1/ 2,110 excluding expatriate community

Table III-8
INDICATORS OF MARKET SIZE:
ASSOCIATION OF SOUTH-EAST ASIAN NATIONS (ASEAN)

	GDP in local currency	GDP in Manufacturing	%	GDP in Construction	%	GDP in Agriculture	%
Indonesia	19,047 1000 million rupiahs (1977)	1,810	10%	912	5%	5,968	31%
Malaysia	17,014 1/ million ringgits (1974)	2,875	17%	863	5%	5,522	32%
Philippines	153,138 million pesos (1977)	37,834	25%	11,356	7%	43,031	28%
Singapore	14,614.8 million S. dollars (1976)	3,608.4	25%	1,178.5	8%	251.8	2%
Thailand	370,445	71,289	19%	21,863	6%	105,445	28%

Note:
1/ At factor cost

Table III-9

INDICATORS OF MARKET SIZE:

ASSOCIATION OF SOUTH-EAST ASIAN NATIONS (ASEAN)

	Employees in manufacturing (%)	Crude steel production (1000 metric tons) Monthly Avgs.	Coal production (1000 metric tons) Monthly Avgs.	Electricity Generated millions of KWH Monthly Avgs.	Railways Freight ton/KLM Monthly Avgs.
Indonesia	(1970) 7%		(1977) 19	(1975) 279	(1977) 71.1 4/
Malaysia	(1970) 8%	(1974) 110		(1977) 600	(1977) 101.0 4/
Philippines	(1977) 132.1 1/		(1977) 23.4	(1977) 951	(1977) 4.0
Singapore	(1976) 27%	(1974) 16.75 2/		(1977) 426 3/	(1977) 101.0 4/
Thailand	(1976) 11%	(1976) 163	(1975) 34.3 2/	(1976) 858	(1976) 219
TOTALS				3,114	395.1

Notes:

1/ Index number of employment in manufacturing, 1970 = 100
2/ Brown coal and lignite
3/ Excludes generation of electricity by industry for own use
4/ Peninsular Malaysia only plus Singapore
5/ Ingot steel

TABLE III-10
INDICATORS OF MARKET SIZE:
CARIBBEAN COMMON MARKET (CARICOM)

	Total GNP at market prices 1976 (US $ in millions)	GNP per capita at market prices 1976 (US $)	Average Annual GNP per capita growth rate 1960-1976	Population mid-1976 (000)	Average Annual population growth rate 1970-1976
Antigua	50	700	-0.2	71	1.7
Barbados	400	1,620	5.1	247	0.6
Belize	100	790	2.7	129	1.1
Dominica	30	370	-0.3	77	1.9
Grenada	50	410	1.9	110	3.0
Guyana	460	570	1.7	793	1.8
Jamaica	2,390	1,150	2.5	2,072	1.8
Montserrat				12.2	
St. Lucia	60	540	2.8	112	2.0
St. Vincent	30	330	0.2	106	2.8
Trinidad & Tobago	2,400	2,190	1.6	1,098	1.1
TOTALS	5,970	1,239		4,827.2	

Table III-11
INDICATORS OF MARKET SIZE:

CARIBBEAN COMMON MARKET (CARICOM)

	GDP in local currency	GDP in Manufacturing	%	GDP in Construction	%	GDP in Agriculture	%
Antigua	92.1 1/ million E.C. dollars	7.2 2/ (1973)	8%	8.0	9%	3.5	4
Barbados	759 million B. dollars	78 (1976)	10%	44	6%	81	10%
Belize	185.4 million B. dollars	18.7 (1976)	10%	13	7%	39	21%
Dominica	62.3 million E.C. dollars	1.0 (1973)	2%	2.3	4%	24.2	39%
Grenada	80.5 1/ million E.C. dollars	3.6 (1975)	5%	5.7	7%	23.1	28%
Guyana	1,117.5 million G. dollars	134.9 3/ (1976)	12%	85	8%	236	21%
Jamaica	2,768 million J. 1/ dollars	539.1 (1976)	19%	257.8	9%	229	8%
Montserrat	16.9 1/ million E.C. dollars	0.3 (1976)	2%	3.5	20%	1.6	9%
St. Lucia	72.8 1/ million E.C. dollars	2.9 4/ (1973)	4%	7.4	10%	13.3	18%
St. Vincent	41.4 1/ million E.C. dollars	1.5 2/ (1972)	4%	4.2	10%	10.5	25%
Trinidad & Tobago	5,607 1/ million T.T. dollars	866 (1976)	15%	318	6%	145	3%

Note: 1/ At factor costs   3/ Includes electricity, gas, and water
      2/ Includes mining   4/ Includes mining, electricity, gas, and water

Table III-12
INDICATORS OF MARKET SIZE:

CARIBBEAN COMMON MARKET (CARICOM)

	Employees in manufacturing (%)	Crude steel production (1000 metric tons) Monthly Avgs.	Coal production (1000 metric tons) Monthly Avgs.	Electricity Generated millions of KWH Monthly Avgs.	Railways Freight ton/KLM Monthly Avgs.
Antigua					
Barbados	(1970) 13%				
Belize	(1970) 21%				
Dominica					
Grenada					
Guyana				(1975) 2 / (1976) 33 / (1977) 117	
Jamaica	(1976) 8%			(1977) 21 1/	(1976) 8.1
Montserrat					
St. Lucia					
St. Vincent					
Trinidad & Tobago	(1975) 19%			(1977) 131	

Note
1/ Production by industry for own use

Table III-13
INDICATORS OF MARKET SIZE:

CENTRAL AMERICAN COMMON MARKET (CACM)

	Total GNP at market prices 1976 (US $ in millions)	GNP per capita at market prices 1976 (US $)	Average Annual GNP per capita growth rate 1960-1976	Population mid-1976 (000)	Average Annual population growth rate 1970-1976
Costa Rica	2,270	1,130	3.3	2,013	2.5
El Salvador	2,190	530	1.8	4,129	3.1
Guatemala	4,390	700	2.8	6,251	2.9
Honduras	1,190	400	1.5	2,959	2.7
Nicaragua	1,800	770	2.6	2,338	3.3
TOTALS	11,840	670		17,690	

Table III-14
INDICATORS OF MARKET SIZE:

CENTRAL AMERICAN COMMON MARKET (CACM)

	GDP in local currency	GDP in Manufacturing	%	GDP in Construction	%	GDP in Agriculture	%
Costa Rica	26,273 million colones (1977)	5,073	19%	1,463	5%	5,840	22%
El Salvador	6,548 million colones (1977)	984	15%	280	4%	1,938	29%
Guatemala	1,262.7 million quetzales (1963)		13%		2%		28%
Honduras	2,940 million lempiras (1977)	457	15%	142	5%	852	29%
Nicaragua	15,691 million cordobas (1977)	2,990	19%	768	5%	3,587	23%

Table III-15
INDICATORS OF MARKET SIZE:

CENTRAL AMERICAN COMMON MARKET (CACM)

	Employees in manufacturing (%)	Crude steel production (1000 metric tons) Monthly Avgs.	Coal production (1000 metric tons) Monthly Avgs.	Electricity Generated millions of KWH Monthly Avgs.	Railways Freight ton/KLM Monthly Avgs.
Costa Rica	(1976) 12%			(1977) 74	(1975) 175.7
El Salvador	(1976) 109.4 1/			(1977) 111	(1975) 33.6
Guatemala	(1976) 85.9 1/			(1976) 88	(1970) 5.5 2/
Honduras	(1976) 8.7			(1975) 40	
Nicaragua	(1976) 9.6			(1975) 77.7	(1976) .72
TOTAL				390.7	

Notes:
1/ Index number of employment in manufacturing, 1970 = 100
2/ Million net ton-miles

Table III-16
INDICATORS OF MARKET SIZE:
COUNCIL OF THE ENTENTE STATES

	Total GNP at market prices 1976 (US $ in millions)	GNP per capita at market prices 1976 (US $)	Average Annual GNP per capita growth rate 1960-1976	Population mid-1976 (000)	Average Annual population growth rate 1970-1976
Benin	570	180	0.0	3,200	1.5
Ivory Coast	4,560	650	3.3	7,025	4.3
Niger	700	150	-1.6	4,730	2.8
Togo	620	270	4.1	2,280	2.6
Upper Volta	640	100	0.6	6,170	2.3
TOTALS	7,090	303		23,405	

Table III-17
INDICATORS OF MARKET SIZE:

COUNCIL OF THE ENTENTE STATES

	GDP in local currency	GDP in Manufacturing	%	GDP in Construction	%	GDP in Agriculture	%
Benin	148.5 1000 million CFA francs (1977)	10.1	6%	4.9	3%	56.5	38%
Ivory Coast	1,582.5 1000 million CFA francs (1977)	183.3	11%	114.2	7%	369.9	23%
Niger	97,808 million CFA francs (1969)	6,282	6%	3,144	3%	50,101	51%
Togo	86,716 million CFA francs (1972)	7,448	8%	4,034	4%	29,560	34%
Upper Volta	109.6 1000 million CFA francs (1974)	11.3	10%	5.3	4%	45.1	41%

Table III-18

INDICATORS OF MARKET SIZE:

COUNCIL OF THE ENTENTE STATES

	Employees in manufacturing (%)	Crude steel production (1000 metric tons) Monthly Avgs.	Coal production (1000 metric tons) Monthly Avgs.	Electricity Generated millions of KWH Monthly Avgs.	Railways Freight ton/KLM Monthly Avgs.
Benin	(1970) 12%			(1975) 4.75	(1977) 11.6
Ivory Coast	(1964) .8%			(1977) 100$\underline{1}$/	(1977) 45.9$\underline{2}$/
Niger	(1970) 2.2%			(1975) 5.8	
Togo				(1976) 6.3	(1976) 3.14$\underline{3}$/
Upper Volta				(1975) 4.38	(1975) 37
TOTALS				121.23	97.64

Notes:

1/ Production by industry for own use

2/ Includes service traffic

3/ Includes passenger baggage, parcel post

Table III-19

INDICATORS OF MARKET SIZE:

EAST AFRICAN COMMON MARKET (EACM)

	Total GNP at market prices 1976 (US $ in millions)	GNP per capita at market prices 1976 (US $)	Average Annual GNP per capita growth rate 1960-1976	Population mid-1976 (000)	Average Annual population growth rate 1970-1976
Kenya	3,460	250	2.6	13,850	3.5
Tanzania	2,770 1/	180 1/	2.6 1/	15,136 1/	2.7 1/
Uganda	3,020	250	1.0	11,937	3.3
TOTALS	9,250	226		40,923	

Note:
1/ Mainland

Table III-20
INDICATORS OF MARKET SIZE:

EAST AFRICAN COMMON MARKET (EACM)

	GDP in local currency	GDP in Manufacturing	%	GDP in Construction	%	GDP in Agriculture	%
Kenya	1,833 million K pounds (1977)	205.4	11%	77.8	4%	620.9	34%
Tanzania	28,270 million K pounds (1977)	2,416	9%	759	3%	12,500	44%
Uganda	10,367 million shillings (1971)	800	8%	195	2%	5,471	53%

Table III-21
INDICATORS OF MARKET SIZE:

EAST AFRICAN COMMON MARKET (EACM)

	Index number manufacturing employment 1970 = 100	Crude steel production (1000 metric tons) Monthly Avgs.	Coal production (1000 metric tons) Monthly Avgs.	Electricity Generated millions of KWH Monthly Avgs.	Railways Freight ton/KLM Monthly Avgs.
Kenya	(1976) 87			(1977) 108	
Tanzania	(1976) 51			(1976) 51	
Uganda	(1976) 58			(1976) 57	
TOTALS				216	(1974) 258

Table III-22
INDICATORS OF MARKET SIZE:

EUROPEAN ECONOMIC COMMUNITY (EEC)

	Total GNP at market prices 1976 (US $ in millions)	GNP per capita at market prices 1976 (US $)	Average Annual GNP per capita growth rate 1960-1976	Population mid-1976 (000)	Average Annual population growth rate 1970-1976
Belgium	68,910	7,020	4.1	9,818	0.3
Denmark	39,000	7,690	3.3	5,073	0.5
Federal Republic of Germany	461,810	7,510	3.3	61,513	0.2
France	355,960	6,730	4.3	52,920	0.7
Ireland	8,290	2,620	3.2	3,162	1.2
Italy	180,650	3,220	3.8	56,156	0.8
Luxembourg	2,350	6,570	2.4	358	1.0
Netherlands	91,610	6,650	3.8	13,770	0.9
United Kingdom, Iceland & Ireland	233,550	4,180	2.7	55,886	0.1
TOTALS	1,422,130	5,575		258,656	

Table III-23
INDICATORS OF MARKET SIZE:

EUROPEAN ECONOMIC COMMUNITY (EEC)

	GDP in local currency	GDP in Manufacturing	%	GDP in Construction	%	GDP in Agriculture	%
Belgium	2,604 1000 million francs (1976)	723	28%	195	7%	75	3%
Denmark	174,634 million kroner (1973)	32,641	19%	16,924	10%	10,699	6%
Federal Republic of Germany	1,198.5 1000 million D. mark (1977)	449.8	37%	86.2	7%	33.5	3%
France	1,647.4 1/ 1000 million francs (1976)	445.1	27%	128.5	8%	79.1	5%
Ireland	2,878 1/ million pounds (1974)	-----856 2/	-----856 2/	30%-----	-----	403	14
Italy	142,128 1/ 1000 million lire (1976)	47,890 3/	34%	10,930	8%	11,285	8%
Luxembourg	80,800 million francs (1975)	28,491 3/	35%	9,185	11%	2,794	3%
Netherlands	261,120 million guilders (1977)	65,920 3/	25%	17,110	6%	10,970	4%
United Kingdom, Iceland & Ireland	121,978 million pounds (1976)	30,464	25%	7,793	6%	3,116	2%

Notes:
1/ Not strictly comparable to other GDP data
2/ Also includes mining, electricity, gas, and water
3/ Includes mining

Table III-24
INDICATORS OF MARKET SIZE:

EUROPEAN ECONOMIC COMMUNITY (EEC)

	Index number manufacturing employment 1970 = 100	Crude steel production (1000 metric tons) Monthly Avgs.	Coal production (1000 metric tons) Monthly Avgs.	Electricity Generated millions of KWH Monthly Avgs.	Railways Freight ton/KLM Monthly Avgs.
Belgium	(1975) 30% 8/	(1977) 939	(1977) 589	(1977) 3,925	(1977) 539 3/
Denmark	(1977) 88	(1977) 57		(1977) 1,874	(1977) 160 4/
Federal Rep. of Germany	(1977) 89.8	(1977) 3,249	(1977) 7,070 1/	(1977) 27,943	(1977) 4,646
France	(1977) 98.7	(1977) 1,842	(1977) 1,774	(1977) 17,529	(1977) 5,519 5/
Ireland	(1977) 98.9	(1976) 58	(1977) 4	(1977) 776	(1977) 44.5
Italy	(1977) 112.9	(1977) 1,942	(1972) 12.6	(1977) 13,881	(1977) 1,343 6/
Luxembourg	(1970) 34% 8/	(1977) 361		(1977) 109	(1977) 47.2
Netherlands	(1977) 84	(1977) 410	(1974) 63	(1977) 4,858	(1977) 234
United Kingdom, Iceland & Ireland	(1977) 88.2	(1977) 1,811	(1977) 10,186 2/	(1977) 23,623	(1977) 1,894 7/
TOTALS		10,669	19,698.6	94,518	14,426.7

Notes:
1/ Excludes 4 percent low grade coal
2/ Includes slurries
3/ Full carloads only
4/ State railways, includes passenger baggage, parcel post, and mail
5/ Includes passenger baggage
6/ Excludes livestock
7/ Excludes Northern Ireland
8/ Percent employed in manufacturing

Table III-25
INDICATORS OF MARKET SIZE:

COUNTRIES WITH SPECIAL ASSOCIATIONS WITH THE EEC

	Total GNP at market prices 1976 (US $ in millions)	GNP per capita at market prices 1976 (US $)	Average Annual GNP per capita growth rate 1960-1976	Population mid-1976 (000)	Average Annual population growth rate 1970-1976
Algeria	16,700	1,010	1.8	16,463	3.5
Cyprus	970	1,520	4.6	640	0.1
Greece	23,600	2,570	6.4	9,169	0.7
Israel	9,710	2,810	5.1	3,460	3.0
Malta & Gozo	560	1,680	7.4	332	0.3
Morocco	8,900	520	2.1	17,197	2.5
Portugal	16,100	1,660	6.2	9,694	1.4
Spain	107,160	2,990	5.4	35,846	1.1
Turkey	41,270	1,010	4.1	40,930	2.5
TOTALS	224,970	1,682		133,731	

Table III-26
INDICATORS OF MARKET SIZE:

COUNTRIES WITH SPECIAL ASSOCIATIONS WITH THE EEC

	GDP in local currency	GDP in Manufacturing	%	GDP in Construction	%	GDP in Agriculture	%
Algeria	68,690 million A. dinars (1976)	9,017	13%	9,164	13%	5,214	8%
Cyprus	425.3 million pounds (1977)	67	16%	25.8	6%	56.4	13%
Greece	813.7 1000 million drachmas (1976)	142.3	17%	52.8	7%	135.1	17%
Israel	76,847 1/ million I. pounds (1976)	23,255 2/	30%	7,815 3/	10%	5,612	7%
Malta & Gozo	203.7 million pounds (1976)	61.5	30%			11.4	6%
Morocco	15.0 1000 million dirhams (1975)		15%		9%		24%
Portugal	464.7 1000 million escudos (1976)	142.8	31%	24.2	5%	61.0	13%
Spain	5,910 1000 million pesetas (1975)	1,571	27%	492	8%	547	9%
Turkey	659 1000 million liras (1976)	120.9	18%	32.2	5%	180.1	27%

Note:
1/ Net domestic product at factory cost
2/ Includes mining
3/ Includes electricity, gas, and water

Table III-27

INDICATORS OF MARKET SIZE:

COUNTRIES WITH SPECIAL ASSOCIATIONS WITH THE EEC

	Index number manufacturing employment 1970 = 100	Crude steel production (1000 metric tons) Monthly Avgs.	Coal production (1000 metric tons) Monthly Avgs.	Electricity Generated millions of KWH Monthly Avgs.	Railways Freight ton/KLM Monthly Avgs.
Algeria	(1966) 7.1%1/	(1974) 15	(1975) .66	(1976) 330	(1976) 143.9
Cyprus	(1976) 13.8%1/			(1977) 74	
Greece	(1977) 132.3	(1976) 800	(1974) 1,615 5/	(1977) 1,450	(1977) 71.3
Israel	(1977) 119.8	(1976) 70		(1977) 926	(1976) 37.4
Malta & Gozo	(1976) 30%1/	(1975) 1 2/		(1977) 354 4/	
Morocco	(1971) 10%1/		(1977) 59	(1977) 287 4/	(1977) 290
Portugal	(1975) 24%1/	(1977) 32	(1977) 16	(1977) 1,156	(1977) 73.7
Spain	(1976) 115.8	(1977) 911	(1977) 976 3/	(1977) 7,809	(1977) 952
Turkey	(1975) 7.6%1/	(1977) 116	(1976) 386	(1977) 1,710	(1977) 531
TOTALS		1,945	1,437.66	13,777	

Notes:

1/ Percent employees in manufacturing
2/ For casting only
3/ Including slurries
4/ Does Not include industrial production for its own use
5/ Coal and Lignite

Table III-28

INDICATORS OF MARKET SIZE:

EUROPEAN FREE TRADE ASSOCIATION (EFTA)

	Total GNP at market prices 1976 (US $ in millions)	GNP per capita at market prices 1976 (US $)	Average Annual GNP per capita growth rate 1960-1976	Population mid-1976 (000)	Average Annual population growth rate 1970-1976
Austria	42,240	5,620	4.3	7,513	0.2
Iceland	930	4,220	3.2	220	1.3
Norway	31,390	7,800	3.9	4,027	0.6
Portugal	16,100	1,660	6.2	9,694	1.4
Sweden	74,220	9,030	3.0	8,219	0.3
Switzerland	58,130	9,160	2.3	6,350	-0.2
Associate Member:					
Finland	27,830	5,890	4.4	4,729	0.5
TOTALS	250,840	6,155		40,752	

Table III-29

INDICATORS OF MARKET SIZE:

EUROPEAN FREE TRADE ASSOCIATION (EFTA)

	GDP in local currency	GDP in Manufacturing	%	GDP in Construction	%	GDP in Agriculture	%
Austria	728.7 1000 million schillings (1976)	230.1 1/	32%	68.8	9%	36.9	5%
Iceland	1.4 US $ billion (1976)						
Iceland	189,474 million kroner (1977)	36,968	20%	14,615	8%	10,766	6%
Portugal	464.7 1000 million escudos (1976)	142.8	31%	24.2	5%	61.0	13%
Sweden	323,278 million kroner (1976)	85,717	26%	20,249	6%	14,365	4%
Switzerland	142,885 million Swiss francs (1976)						
Associate Member: Finland	121,557 million markkaa (1977)	33,038	27%	9,980	8%	11,653	10%

Note:
1/ Includes mining

Table III-30

INDICATORS OF MARKET SIZE:

EUROPEAN FREE TRADE ASSOCIATION (EFTA)

	Index number manufacturing employment 1970 = 100	Crude steel production (1000 metric tons) Monthly Avgs.	Coal production (1000 metric tons) Monthly Avgs.	Electricity Generated millions of KWH Monthly Avgs.	Railways Freight ton/KLM Monthly Avgs.
Austria	(1977) 100.8	(1977) 358	(1976) 268 3/	(1977) 3,140	(1977) 817 6/
Iceland	(1974) 24% 1/			(1977) 217 5/	
Norway	(1977) 105.1	(1977) 61	(1977) 38 4/	(1977) 6,041	(1977) 219
Portugal	(1975) 24% 1/	(1977) 32	(1977) 16	(1977) 1,156	(1977) 73 7/
Sweden	(1977) 101.2	(1977) 330	(1976) 12	(1977) 7,298	(1977) 1,232 8/
Switzerland	(1977) 79.6	(1976) 545		(1977) 3,677	(1977) 494 8/
Associate Member:					
Finland	(1977) 105.4	(1977) 183		(1977) 2,656	(1977) 533
TOTALS		1,509		24,185	

Notes:

1/ Percent employed in manufacturing, also including mining and quarrying

2/ Percent employed in manufacturing

3/ Brown coal and lignite

4/ Norwegian operated mines only

5/ Not including production by industrial establishments primarily for their own use

6/ Federal railways, full carloads only

7/ State railways only

8/ Federal railways only

Table III-31
INDICATORS OF MARKET SIZE:
LATIN AMERICAN FREE TRADE ASSOCIATION (LAFTA)

	Total GNP at market prices 1976 (US $ in millions)	GNP per capita at market prices 1976 (US $)	Average Annual GNP per capita growth rate 1960-1976	Population mid-1976 (000)	Average Annual population growth rate 1970-1976
Argentina	40,730	1,580	2.9	25,710	1.3
Bolivia	2,970	510	2.3	5,794	2.7
Brazil	143,000	1,300	4.8	110,124	2.8
Chile	10,870	1,050	1.1	10,375	1.8
Colombia	15,740	650	2.7	24,301	2.8
Ecuador	5,100	700	3.0 1/	7,306	3.5
Mexico	65,460	1,060	3.0	62,025	3.5
Paraguay	1,700	650	2.2	2,625	2.7
Peru	13,450	840	2.5	16,068	3.0
Uruguay	3,830	1,370	0.7	2,800	0.5
Venezuela	31,340	2,540	2.6	12,361	3.1
TOTALS	334,190	1,196		279,498	

Note:
1/ 1965-1976

Table III-32
INDICATORS OF MARKET SIZE:

LATIN AMERICAN FREE TRADE ASSOCIATION (LAFTA)

	GDP in local currency	GDP in Manufacturing	%	GDP in Construction	%	GDP in Agriculture	%
Argentina	1,345 1000 million pesos (1975)	448.1	33%	54.7	4%	164.3	12%
Bolivia	50,156 million pesos (1975)	6,603	13%	2,154	4%	9,022	18%
Brazil	2,352,775 million cruzeiros (1977)	543,833	23%	108,889	5%	236,849	10%
Chile	321,188 million pesos (1977)	65,468	20%	6,315	2%	33,011	10%
Colombia	419,013 million pesos (1975)	91,927	22%	20,165	5%	114,180	27%
Ecuador	153,812 million sucres (1977)	25,748	17%	9,671	6%	31,279	20%
Mexico	1,220.8 1000 million pesos (1976)	298.6	24%	74.9	6%	110.3	9%
Paraguay	263,612 million guaranies (1977)	44,974	17%	10,560	4%	89.925	34%
Peru	827.7 1000 million soles (1976)	235.5	28%	33.2	4%	105.6	13%
Uruguay	12,537.1 million new pesos (1976)	3,102.6	25%	423.9	3%	1,227.1	10%
Venezuela	152,796 million bolivares (1977)	24,972	16%	10,689	7%	9,527	6%

Table III-33
INDICATORS OF MARKET SIZE:

LATIN AMERICAN FREE TRADE ASSOCIATION (LAFTA)

	Employees in manufacturing (%)	Crude steel production (1000 metric tons) Monthly Avgs.	Coal production (1000 metric tons) Monthly Avgs.	Electricity Generated millions of KWH Monthly Avgs.	Railways Freight ton/KLM Monthly Avgs.
Argentina	(1975) 20%	(1977) 223	(1977) 44	(1977) 2,278	(1977) 964
Bolivia				(1975) 83.3	
Brazil	(1970) 11%	(1977) 931	(1977) 292 4/	(1976) 7,365	(1973) 2,210 6/
Chile	(1977) 93.9 1/	(1977) 42 2/	(1977) 103	(1977) 822	(1977) 184
Colombia	(1977) 122.3 1/	(1977) 18	(1976) 3,620	(1977) 1,118	(1977) 101.3 5/
Ecuador	(1975) 120.7			(1975) 107.5	(1975) 3.85
Mexico	(1976) 18%	(1977) 451	(1976) 5,650	(1977) 4,171	(1977) 3,019
Paraguay	(1972) 15%			(1975) 44	(1973) 1.6 6/
Peru	(1972) 13%	(1976) 349 3/	(1973) 10	(1977) 275	(1976) 63
Uruguay	(1975) 19%	(1976) 15		(1976) 233	(1976) 27
Venezuela	(1977) 139.8	(1977) 68	(1977) 10.1	(1976) 1,939.7	(1971) .77 6/
TOTAL				18,436.5	

Notes:

1/ Index number of employment in manufacturing, 1970 = 100

2/ Ingots only

3/ For casting only

4/ Including waste

5/ Including service traffic

6/ Million net ton-miles

Table III-34
INDICATORS OF MARKET SIZE:

MAGHREB GROUP

	Total GNP at market prices 1976 (US $ in millions)	GNP per capita at market prices 1976 (US $)	Average Annual GNP per capita growth rate 1960-1976	Population mid-1976 (000)	Average Annual population growth rate 1970-1976
Algeria	16,700	1,101	1.8	16,463	3.5
Morocco	8,900	520	2.1	17,197	2.5
Tunisia	4,580	800	4.2	5,732	2.4
TOTALS	30,180	766		39,392	

Table III-35
INDICATORS OF MARKET SIZE:

MAGHREB GROUP

	GDP in local currency	GDP in Manufacturing	%	GDP in Construction	%	GDP in Agriculture	%
Algeria	68,690 million A. dinars (1976)	9,107	13%	9,164	15%	5,214	8%
Morocco	15.0 1000 million dirhams (1975)	15%		9%		24%	
Tunisia	1,744.2 154.8 million dinars (1975)	154.8	9%	136.3	8%	311.7	18%

Table III-36
INDICATORS OF MARKET SIZE:

MAGHREB GROUP

	Employees in manufacturing (%)	Crude steel production (1000 metric tons) Monthly Avgs.	Coal production (1000 metric tons) Monthly Avgs.	Electricity Generated millions of KWH Monthly Avgs.	Railways Freight ton/KLM Monthly Avgs.
Algeria	(1966) 7.1%	(1974) 15 1/	(1975) .66	(1976) 330	(1976) 143.9
Morocco	(1971) 10%	(1975) 1 1/	(1977) 59	(1977) 287	(1977) 290
Tunisia	(1974) 13.5%	(1976) 103 1/		(1977) 127	(1977) 110.9 2/
TOTALS		119	59.66	744	

Notes:
1/ Crude steel for casting only
2/ Includes service traffic

Table III-37
INDICATORS OF MARKET SIZE:

UNION OF CENTRAL AFRICAN STATES (UDEAC)

	Total GNP at market prices 1976 (US $ in millions)	GNP per capita at market prices 1976 (US $)	Average Annual GNP per capita growth rate 1960-1976	Population mid-1976 (000)	Average Annual population growth rate 1970-1976
Cameroon	2,380	310	3.0	7,606	1.9
Central African Empire	430	240 1/	0.3 1/	1,827	2.2
Congo	730	530	1.3	1,360	2.3
Gabon	2,050	3,780	6.7	544	1.7
TOTALS	3,520	310		11,337	

Note:
1/ Tentative

Table III-38

INDICATORS OF MARKET SIZE:

UNION OF CENTRAL AFRICAN STATES (UDEAC)

	GDP in local currency	GDP in Manufacturing	%	GDP in Construction	%	GDP in Agriculture	%
Cameroon	790.9 1000 million CFA francs (1976)	83.6	11%	47.0	6%	245.1	31%
Central African Empire	57.1 1000 million CFA francs (1971)	5.4	9%	1.8	3%	18.4	32%
Congo	500 US $ million (1974)						
Gabon	462.4 1000 million CFA francs (1975)	23.0	4%	79.8	17	40.8	8%

Table III-39

INDICATORS OF MARKET SIZE:

UNION OF CENTRAL AFRICAN STATES (UDEAC)

	Employees in manufacturing (%)	Crude steel production (1000 metric tons) Monthly Avgs.	Coal production (1000 metric tons) Monthly Avgs.	Electricity Generated millions of KWH Monthly Avgs.	Railways Freight ton/KLM Monthly Avgs.
Cameroon	15.9%			(1976) 111 2/	(1974/75) 33.3
Central African Empire				(1975) 4.33	
Congo				(1977) 10	(1977) 42.4
Gabon	(1972) 2% 1/			(1976) 19 3/	
TOTAL				144.33	

Notes:
1/ Includes industry and commerce
2/ Includes production by industrial establishments primarily for their own use
3/ Industrial production for own use negligible

Table III-40

INDICATORS OF MARKET SIZE:

WEST AFRICAN ECONOMIC COMMUNITY (CEAO)

	Total GNP at market prices 1976 (US $ in millions)	GNP per capita at market prices 1976 (US $)	Average Annual GNP per capita growth rate 1960-1976	Population mid-1976 (000)	Average Annual population growth rate 1970-1976
Benin	570	180	0.3	3,200	1.5
Ivory Coast	4,560	650	3.3	7,025	4.3
Mali	600	100	0.9	5,840	2.5
Mauritania	250	380	3.7	1,495	2.4
Niger	700	150	-1.6	4,730	2.8
Senegal	2,110	410	-0.4	5,135	2.7
Upper Volta	640	100	0.6	6,170	2.3
TOTALS	9,430	281		33,595	

Table III-41
INDICATORS OF MARKET SIZE:

WEST AFRICAN ECONOMIC COMMUNITY (CEAO)

	GDP in local currency	GDP in Manufacturing	%	GDP in Construction	%	GDP in Agriculture	%
Benin	148.5 1000 million CFA francs (1977)	(10.1) [1]/	6%	4.9	3%	56.5	38%
Ivory Coast	1,582.5 1000 million CFA francs (1977)	183.3	11%	114.2	7%	369.9	23%
Mali	.32 US $ million (1971)						
Mauritania	13,043 million ouguiyas (1973)	623	5%	615	5%	2,921	22%
Niger	97,808 million CFA francs (1969)	628.2	6%	3,144	3%	50,101	51%
Senegal	1.57 US $ billion (1975)						
Upper Volta	109.6 1000 million CFA francs (1974)	11.3	10%	5.3	4%	45.1	41%

Note
1/ Includes mining

Table III-42

INDICATORS OF MARKET SIZE:

WEST AFRICAN ECONOMIC COMMUNITY (CEAO)

	Employees in manufacturing (%)	Crude steel production (1000 metric tons) Monthly Avgs.	Coal production (1000 metric tons) Monthly Avgs.	Electricity Generated millions of KWH Monthly Avgs.	Railways Freight ton/KLM Monthly Avgs.
Benin	(1970) 12%4/			(1975) 4.75	(1977) 11.6
Ivory Coast	(1964) .8%			(1977) 100 1/	(1977) 45.9 2/
Mali	(1970) 4.1%			(1975) 5.8	(1977) 12.4
Mauritania				(1977) 8.0	
Niger	(1970) 2.2%			(1975) 5.8	352.3 3/
Senegal	(1970) 6.5%			(1976) 38	(1976) 13.7
Upper Volta				(1975) 4.38	(1975) 37
TOTAL				166.73	

Notes:

1/ Industrial production for own use negligible
2/ Includes service traffic
3/ Million net ton-miles
4/ Includes mining

Annex IV
Trade Blocs in Latin America: Summary and Analysis

Wilbur F. Monroe

I. Growth in Latin American Trade Blocs

A. <u>Trade Blocs in Latin America</u>. Four regional trade blocs have arisen in Latin America -- all since 1960. The first and biggest bloc is the Latin America Free Trade Association (LAFTA). It was established in 1960 as a free trade area, encompassing almost all of the Latin American countries with the exception of the Central American countries, the Caribbean countries, and Guyana.

The second trade bloc is known as the Central American Common Market (CACM). It also was set up in 1960, but as a common market, meaning the establishment of a common tariff wall between the area and the rest of the world in addition to the establishment of free trade between members. Five countries are members: Guatemala, El Salvador, Honduras, Costa Rica, and Nicaragua.

The third is the Andean Common Market (ANCOM). It was established in 1969 as an offshoot of LAFTA. Essentially, the ANCOM countries are weaker economically than others comprising LAFTA. Members felt they could do better on their own rather than trying to integrate with other stronger countries, and so broke away. Countries included in ANCOM are Peru, Chile, Bolivia, Ecuador, and Colombia. Later, Venezuela joined, and Chile dropped out after President Allende's demise.

The fourth bloc is the Caribbean Economic Community (CARICOM). It began in 1973 as a free trade zone, but it is now organized as a common market. It grew out of the Caribbean Free Trade Association (CARIFTA), which originated in 1965. Members include Grenada, Barbados, Jamaica, and Guyana.

The original goal of the trade bloc movement in Latin America was to realize a single Latin American Common Market from the Rio Grande to Cape Horn. In fact, during meetings resulting in the Accord of Montevideo of 1967, in which the United States participated, it was verbalized that the goal was a "Latin American Common Market" (LACM) by 1980. These aspirations have been sidetracked for a number of reasons to be discussed below, and the main thought at present is to realize a "preferential zone" by 1980. The intent is that member countries will try to give preference to one another. However, there is no statement as to what such preference is to include, nor to what lengths members will go to extend such preference. It remains a vague and very general concept.

All four of the above-mentioned trade blocs continue to exist. In addition, Cuba has been a member of COMECON, the European Communist trade bloc, since the early 1960s, and it remains so today.

B. Why Trade Blocs Were Formed and What They Have Achieved. Latin America embraced the concept of trade blocs because it was seen as an aid to stimulating and achieving economic development. This contrasts with what occurred in Western Europe where trade blocs were viewed as a device for heightening economic efficiency. Leaders in Latin America hoped that trade blocs would help break down barriers to intra-regional trade. Their thought was that investment in manufacturing enterprises would be substantially increased as a consequence of such trade. A chief characteristic of industry is that of decreasing costs of production, which puts a premium on volume output. Thus, if single-country markets could be broadened by removing trade barriers, industry would develop. What they had in mind, however, was indigenous investment. Of course, investment from foreign sources could be stimulated as well, but this was not what the leadership talked about.

For Latin America as a whole, there was some trade liberalization, especially in the early years. The volume of intra-regional trade as a percentage of total foreign trade of Latin America rose from 15 percent in 1960 to about 18 percent in 1966. This modest gain from a small beginning points up to the fact that Latin American countries trade very little among each other, before as well as at present. The chief reason is that little economic complimentarity exists between countries. That is to say, many of the same basic products are produced in each country. From the time trade blocs in Latin America began, various problems were encountered. In the case of LAFTA (the largest bloc), and in general for Latin

America, there were two fundamental problems. First, in a political sense, the leadership of any given country was unwilling to make concessions in the name of advancing broader interests. Quite simply, the price of such concessions was expressed in short-term respects (outcry of the local opposition), while economic benefits could be expected to appear only in the long-term. Second, there was a tendency toward economic polarization. To the extent that new investments occurred and industries arose, growth took place, by and large, in those locales that were relatively strong in economic terms (São Paulo, Buenos Aires, Mexico City, so forth). This was a basic reason why poorer countries (ANCOM) became alienated and split away from LAFTA.

CACM has fared better than other trade blocs in Latin America. This conclusion follows from a number of meaningful tests that might be applied. The explanation is that its members, although weak economically, were the most similar. This bloc has been able to attract foreign companies (many of them U.S. firms) to establish assembly and packaging operations within their borders. But CACM has encountered very limited success since 1969, at which point the famous "soccer war" occurred between El Salvador and Honduras. These two countries do not trade with each other even now.

When ANCOM was set up, it had somewhat different goals from the other blocs. The three main objectives were trade liberalization (as with LAFTA), some procedures to help locate new industry in order to prevent polarization, and -- most important -- foreign investment guidelines. The Andean Investment Code, which still exists, deals with what to expect from new investments, how to treat already established investments, what to do when investment problems arise, and procedures for expropriation.

Countries belonging to CARICOM are strongly oriented toward tourism. Little industry apart from that exists, and agriculture is generally inefficient, except for Guyana. The absence of a common agricultural policy has been a problem, but beyond that, there has been little potential for common market objectives to be exercised.

II. Impact of Latin American Trade Blocs

The "trade bloc" movements in Latin America have had no more than a marginal effect on U.S. business activities. These activities (trade, investment flows, licensing) have undergone shifts and trends, but this has occurred for more general economic and political reasons than for reasons directly related to the presence or absence of "trade bloc" movements.

A. Exports From the United States. U.S. merchandise exports to Latin America have risen five-fold in dollar value over the past 20 years. In share of total world merchandise exports to Latin America, however, the United States has declined; the United States had a 35 percent share in 1960 and a 25 percent share in 1977-78. In contrast, Japan rose from a 3 percent share in 1960 to 9 percent in 1977-78, and the EEC countries rose in the same period from about 15 percent to around 20 percent. In regard to manufactured goods exports to Latin America, the U.S. total rose less than three-fold. Japan's exports of such goods, however, rose about five-fold. Thus, the slippage of the U.S. share is more pronounced in the manufactures category than it is in the aggregate.

B. Direct Investment in Manufacturing. While Latin America did not talk much about the potential for inducing foreign investment inflows by using the common market attraction, there were some positive effects. These occurred largely in the realm of assembly and packaging operations, particularly in Central America.

But the predominant trends related far more directly to other factors. What happened for other reasons were as follows. First, gyrations in the political climate in Latin America were reflected in an uneven pace of direct investment inflow. For instance, the Cuban case at the outset of the 1960s had a very detrimental impact on U.S. investment flows all over the region. Second, the investment inflow into Latin America has been characterized by a movement more to Japanese and EEC sources and to a lesser relative reliance on U.S. sources. Third, the most recent outstanding feature in foreign investment is the entry of multinational bank lending operations. Lending in various forms has become a competitor of direct investment. Japanese and EEC bank lending operations have been expanding faster than U.S. bank lending. Most pronounced is the case of Japan, ostensibly because Japanese banks cooperate very

closely with Japanese firms and with their business
dealings in Latin America and elsewhere. Fourth,
the foreign direct investment inflows and the multinational bank loans are entering on a "spotty" basis.
That is to say, some countries receive substantial
amounts while others get hardly anything. The
general picture is that the larger, stronger countries
fare best. It has very little to do with whether a
given country is in a trade bloc, or in one particular
trade bloc as opposed to another.

C. Licensing Activities. There are three major
trends in this area. First, and in general, licensing
has been growing up to the present for the United
States, Japan, and the EEC. Second, Japan has done
particularly well. There seems to be considerable
appeal in Latin America for that country's technology.
Japanese aggressiveness is also important. But there
is discernible pique at the United States by many
Latin Americans as well. (Given a trade-off, a Latin
American businessman or government official may very
well choose a non-U.S. supplier.) Third, as direct
investment has slowed, licensing seems to slow also.
This suggests that foreign companies made their
investments, setting up subsidiaries in the foreign
country, and then licensing know-how to those subsidiaries. However, with the recent apparent slowing
of growth in direct investment, it is worth mentioning
that direct investment may be offset by willingness to
license to foreign firms other than one's own subsidiaries. But Latin America has become disenchanted
with some licensing arrangements in recent years.
Countries have imposed restrictions, believing previous arrangements have been very costly. Also, the
complaint is made that the foreign parent licenses its
local subsidiaries in preference to indigenous enterprises.

III. Latin America as a Trade Bloc

Latin America should appropriately be regarded
as a "trade bloc." In the global context, there is
no economic rationale for there being four blocs
within Latin America.
Within the Latin America "trade bloc," the United
States is losing ground to other countries in relative
terms. Japan is the prime beneficiary, and the EEC
also, but to a lesser extent. Why is Latin America
shifting away from the United States? First, there
is considerable disillusionment with this country.
For years, the United States neglected the "special

relationship," and now Latin America is looking elsewhere. (The news reports about President Carter's
visit to Mexico in February 1979 reflect this
feeling.) Second, Japan's technology is attractive
to Latin American countries, and the Japanese market
their know-how aggressively and effectively. Third,
Latin America has been historically part of the
dollar area. But the value of their dollar reserves
has been eroding in recent years, a fact which has
not been lost on responsible Latin American money
managers. The Deutsche Mark, the yen, and the Swiss
franc have more appeal now.

IV. Highlights of the Literature

A. Latin American Trade Blocs

1. Walter Krause and F. John Mathis, Latin
America and Economic Integration, University of Iowa Press, 1970.

2. Ronald Hilton, ed., The Movement Toward
Latin Unity, Praeger Press, 1969.

3. William R. Cline and Enrique Delgado,
eds., Economic Integration in Central
America, The Brookings Institution, 1978.

B. Data Sources on Trade

1. U.N. Statistical Yearbook

2. GATT, Directions of Trade

C. Investment

1. Albert O. Hirschman, How to Divest in
Latin America and Why, Princeton Series,
1969 (Includes Andean Investment Code).

2. Osvaldo Sunkel, "Big Business and 'Depen-
dencia:' A Latin American View," Foreign
Affairs, April 1972. (Spells out case
against direct investment.)

3. F. John Mathis, ed., "Offshore Lending
by U.S. Commercial Banks," Bankers'
Association for Foreign Trade, Washington,
1975.

D. Data Sources on Foreign Investment

    1. Department of Commerce, U.S. Survey of Current Business.

    2. OECD, country surveys.

E. Licensing

    1. Business International loose leaf series.

    2. Prentice Hall loose leaf series.

Annex V
The Effectiveness, Growth, and Impact of Economic Organizations as They Exist in Africa

Tamburai M'ndange-Pfupfu

> Why is Africa shaped like a question mark?
> Africa must have the answer. Supposedly the
> first human being roamed the plains of Africa
> many millions of years ago. Perhaps through
> economic integration, we can pool human
> resources, learn the art of distributing the
> gifts of this world, and grow to be neighbors.

The African desire for economic cooperation stretches bank to colonial days or earlier. Today it acquires special significance for a number of reasons. 1) A large portion of the African population is below subsistence level; 2) the level of industrial development is very low in comparison with other countries of the world -- also, agriculture predominates both in overall economic activities and in the volume and value of exports; and, 3) an underdeveloped traditional rural sector exists side by side with a relatively advanced urban sector and the low general rate of economic development in the agriculture sector tends to slow the overall rate of development.

Taking the above factors together, an African country would have to expend vast capital and technical resources to achieve and sustain a minimum rate of development -- such resources are often beyond the reach of an African country. Under such conditions, the path toward development lies in cooperation at all levels to ensure that the resources are exploited in the best interest of the African countries.

The institutional framework as a colonial legacy in most African countries is responsible for the economic backwardness and slow rate of economic progress, as was the case in the Europe of the 1940s. The need for large applications of capital investment arises as a result of various technical indivisibili-

ties and external economies. Assuming it is possible
for an individual state or multinational company in
a low-income region to undertake large doses of
capital investments, that country or firm is faced
with excess capacity or underutilization of its
plant capacity. Extensive participation in capital
investments by a large number of countries is
recommended in order to avoid excess capacity problems.
The argument is relevant to African countries, as well
as to American investors. Both need a large developed
market. There is considerable excess capacity in most
basic industries in Africa already, and in some cases
production units are operating below 50 percent of
capacity.

Most African countries and economic communities
are ambivalent about expanded domestic output.
Invariably, African countries that organize an economic community and create a potential market want to
protect their young industries and, above all, need
the revenue from common external tariffs. Thus, any
diversion of demand from products manufactured overseas to those manufactured within the economic
community will result in a loss of revenues most of
these countries are reluctant to take, for the sake
of supporting local industries or for the badly
needed foreign investment.

The dilemma of indivisibility of the demand
function has led governments and international agencies
to the large-scale investment of capital over a wide
range of industries and projects. Piecemeal investments will not solve the problems of economic development in Africa. The rate of investment in Africa has
generally been very low anyway, even in comparison
with other developing countries. This low investment
rate has been due to the low savings rate among the
African people, which results from low incomes. The
low incomes are due to low productivity, which results
from the low rate of investment.[1] This vicious
circle is a serious constraint to development.

Various ways of breaking through this vicious
circle have been suggested, and the pros and cons of
the arguments are well-known -- we do not need to go
into them here. What we need to say, though, is that
in order to attract more capital resources, the
African investment market must be made more attractive. Where investment decisions are still governed
largely by profit motives, there is every need to

1/ See: Ragnar Nurkse, Problems of Capital Formation
in Underdeveloped Countries (Oxford: Basil Blackwell,
1962), p. 4.

assure the foreign investors of a fair return on
their capital outlays. Above all, political stability
and tranquility must be seen to exist. Obviously, no
single African country is capable of giving such
guarantees, especially with regard to the establishment of large-scale industries. Only when the
economies are integrated and when risk can be spread
over a wide area will foreign investors be attracted
to invest heavily and on a wider scale.

What has tended to happen as a consequence of
these investment problems, is that direct investments
have taken place in areas with a stable government
and an economic cooperation organization well established. The experience of the former East African
Community is a good example. American direct investments have poured into Kenya mainly for three reasons:
1) The belief among American and British investors
that Kenya was politically stable; 2) Kenya was a
major member of the East African Community and its
per capita income and GNP were the highest of the
three countries; and, 3) above all, there existed a
potential market in the region of Kenya's membership.
After independence, Kenya did not take over the
country's major manufacturing establishments as did
Tanzania immediately after the Arusha Declaration.[2]
Even though no outright confiscation was involved,
and President Nyerere reaffirmed the government
policy that there was room for private investment in
Tanzania, considerable uncertainty persisted and by
the end of 1977, no one knew for sure the extent to
which foreign investment could participate in the
small business sector expansion in Tanzania. There
exists a contradiction in Tanzania's policy regarding
public and private sectors in manufacturing that is
mainly due to the pursuit of socialist goals. We
shall come back to Tanzania's investment policy
later.

Foreign Investment

U.S. total investment interests in the East
African Community were minor -- principally in sales
outlets and shipping line properties. Goods, capital,
and labor could freely flow within the common market
area except in certain industries which each country
was developing domestically. There were Foreign

---

[2] See: Irving Kaplan (ed.), Tanzania: A Country
Study (Area handbook series, Foreign Area Studies, The
American University, Washington, D.C., 1978), p. 213.

Investment Protection Acts and Investment Guarantee
Agreements in force in all three countries. and
foreign private capital was welcome.

East African Aids to
Fostening Private Investment

Development Corporations. While it is true that
both trading partners impose barriers on exports and
imports on each other's country, it is equally true
that both sides provide some incentives to boost
trade between their countries. The United States
enacts laws designed to protect the local consumer
market from exports of consumer goods from Africa.
The Africans on their part, try to protect their
infant consumer industry, their only hope of breaking
the vicious balance of payments problem that continues to erode as more and more prices of the limited
number of export commodities fall.

Kenya. The Development Finance Corporation
organized in 1963, was designed to stimulate the flow
of private investment by providing loans or share
capital to fill marginal gaps in private project
finance. The Kenyan government, Federal Republic of
West Germany, and the United Kingdom, each owned one
third of the shares. The Kenyan government also had
an Industrial Development Corporation, which operated
a fund to provide loans to African industrialists in
Kenya.

Uganda. The government of Uganda operated a
Development Corporation whose main objective was to
further economic and industrial development by participating with Uganda industrialists and foreign
investors already involved in a network of subsidiary
corporations that receive financial and/or technical
assistance from the parent company. The Uganda Development Corporation was a limited liability company in
which the government was the sole shareholder.

Tanganyika. The government of Tanganyika operated the National Development Corporation, which
served as the main initiator of development investment in Tanzania. Here as well, the government was
the sole shareholder.
Each member of the East African economic group
had further aid to foster trade and investment, such
as public financing institutions and government
trading organizations.

Import and Export Controls in
the East African Community

While trading among the countries of the Community was generally unrestricted, import licensing and quota regulations were in force on certain items, particularly in cases where an unfavorable balance of trade existed between two of the member states. However, most imports into Kenya and mainland Tanzania, including those from the United States, were freely admitted under the Open General License - still, each country required a specific import license for certain items. In the case of Uganda, however, there was no general import licensing system. Any nonprohibited goods were either freely admitted, as were most U.S. goods, or required a specific import license. All commercial transactions involving foreign exchange in these countries was subject to control. However, an attempt was made to facilitate the issuance of licenses for goods covered under bilateral trade agreements.

The East African major export commidities during the 1960s were coffee (not roasted), sisal fiber and tow, cotton (raw), tea, and pyrethrum extract. These commodities remain the major export items. When we look at the share of the U.S. - East African trade volume by country in amounts and percentages of the total for the period 1960-64, we find that most exports went to Kenya throughout that 5 year period. From 1963-64, U.S. exports to that country were rising. At the same time, Kenya's exports to the United States were also increasing, but by a smaller percentage. In the same period, Tanganyika imported the second largest amount of U.S. exports while Uganda imported the least. However, taken together, the total imports of U.S. exports to East Africa continued to rise.3/

As was pointed out previously, the United States continued to make strides into the import markets of the individual East African Economic Community member states a decade after the first period we looked at. To drive the point home, we look at trade between the United States and two of these countries in more detail before moving on to a survey of the U.S. trade situation with a West African country in the 1970s.

3/ Source: East African Customs and Excise, EACSO, Annual Trade Report of Tanganyika, Uganda and Kenya, 1964, Mombasa, Kenya; Economic and Statistical Review No. 9, p. 22 and No. 13, p. 20. Table

Kenya. By the end of 1975, the United States had 9 percent of the $833 million market and was Kenya's fourth supplier. The United Kingdom, which has remained a leading investor and supplier, furnished 21 percent and the European Economic Community (EEC) members covered 20 percent of total imports. Iran was the major supplier of crude oil, and West Germany next, supplying 15 percent and 8 percent respectively of Kenya's imports.4/ In 1977, however, U.S. leading principal exports were: aircraft and aircraft parts, road motor vehicles, telecommunications equipment, fertilizer, pesticides and insecticides, cereals (except corn flakes), and agro-industrial machinery. In addition, opportunities existed for sales of World Bank financed projects, including the Integrated Agricultural Development Projects, the Rural Access Roads Project, and the Bura Irrigation Scheme as well as ongoing expansion projects. As a consequence, over 200 U.S. companies established and/or enlarged their operations in recent years. Trade is a two-way street. During the same period, 1976-77, U.S. imports from Kenya also continued to rise.5/

Kenyan Investment Policy

Since independence, the Kenyan government has taken a positive stance toward foreign investment, particularly when there is Kenyan equity participation. To be sure, most foreign investment in the country has been in the area of production of consumer goods and local policy has been increasingly to encourage diversification into higher technology industries. In the mid 1970s, the main source of foreign private investment in Kenya has continued to be the United Kingdom, the former colonial power. There are no reliable figures on total private foreign investment in Kenya available; suffice it to say investment interest on the part of companies in Western Europe and Japan has significantly increased in recent years.

The number of American firms with direct representation in Kenya has risen dramatically from 20 in 1962 to over 200 in 1976. The monetary value of U.S.

4/ For leading U.S. Exports to Kenya during 1972-1975, see: U.S. Bureau of the Census, Ft 455, EQ 455 1972-75 (microfilm).

5/ Table V-1 shows quantity and value of U.S. trade with Kenya in the period 1976-77.

private investment in Kenya is estimated at $150 to
$160 million. With few exceptions, U.S. investments
in Kenya have proven successful. The Kenyan authori-
ties have expressed particular interest in increased
investment for U.S. business as they have been
favorably impressed by U.S. management capabilities.
American firms manufacture batteries, soap products,
and can Kenyan agricultural products for Kenyan
markets and export, among other economic activity.
Included among U.S. firms with major manufacturing
facilities in Kenya are Firestone, Colgate-Palmolive,
Crown Cork, and Del Monte, to name a few.

Tanzania. While there are a number of sectors
ranging from agribusiness and textiles to solar
technology and minerals exploration, the government
of Tanzania is not enamored with foreign investment
as a matter of principle. Thus, the Tanzanians are
quite selective of the types of joint venture proposals they will entertain. In 1978, invariably,
the terms of any foreign investment must be worked
out on an ad hoc basis.

Legally, there are no restrictions on the investment of foreign funds in Tanzania. But the
Foreign Investment Act of 1963 requires that foreign
and domestic investments in specified types of production require approval under the East African
Licensing Ordinance. There is every reason to believe
that this ordinance is being revised, since the break-
up of the East African Economic Community in late
1977.

Tanzania's investment ownership policy falls
into three categories: 1) total public control;
2) partnership between government parastatal corporations; and, 3) privately owned industry by local
and foreign investors. In most of the major or basic
industries, government policy is to acquire a 50 percent share or more. However, an investment legisla-
tion is in force which offers a variety of fiscal
incentives and import duty reliefs as well as exclu-
sive licenses. Furthermore, a Foreign Investment
Protection Act is in existence, which offers guarantees of compensation in the event of expropriation
and remittance of profits. In 1977, an Investment
Guarantee Agreement was signed between Tanzania and
the United States. Thus, for example, the Overseas
Private Investment Corporation (OPIC) extended political risk insurance to an American contracting firm
that was working on a U.S. financed A.I.D. project in
Tanzania. Nevertheless, by December of 1978, there
was very little U.S. investment in Tanzania.

The overall result of this strictly regulated economy with government ownership of means of production and the dominance of parastatal corporations, among other economic reasons, caused severe fluctuating volumes in Tanzanian exports to the United States, while U.S. exports to that country steadily rose.[6] The leading items in the U.S. export bill were spare parts, machinery, and transport equipment. U.S. agribusiness has also been invited to study and invest in establishing large modern farms to product rice, soybeans, and other food crops for the domestic market.

West Africa

When we turn to look at a selected West African state outside any organized economic cooperations, we get the same picture we get from individual countries of East Africa -- investment and trade with the United States is dictated by stable political institutions, a mixed economy capable of sustaining growth, together with liberal terms of trade and licensing policy, and not by the mere existence of an economic customs union.

Ivory Coast. Throughout its 17 years of independence, the primary economic objective of the country has been to maximize growth. This has been based on the belief that, given a historical low level of Ivorian per capita income, expansion much more than income redistribution offers a promising means for improving the living standards of the average Ivorian. To that objective the government promoted the growth of a mixed economy with a dynamic private sector, but also an extensive network of state owned enterprises. In addition the Ivory Coast sought assistance in the form of capital, technology, management skills, and even unskilled labor wherever it could find it. The Ivory Coast stands out among low-income countries in the extent to which it has accepted foreign participation in its economy.

The Ivory Coast's industrial development program as presented in a five year plan in 1978 calls for progress toward establishing a modern competitive and increasingly self-sufficient industrial sector that would reduce Ivorian dependence upon the vagaries of agricultural production and prices. But the success

---

6/ See Table V-2 for U.S. trade with Tanzania during 1976-77.

of the industrial development program depends in large part upon the equity participation of private, particularly foreign, investors. Yet, the public sector is increasingly outdistancing the private in the extent of its investment activities.

Implications for the United States. Similar to the Kenyan situation, France, as a former colonial master, has the largest share of foreign investment in the Ivory Coast. It is the largest supplier and has assumed the major responsibility for assisting the Ivory Coast's development. Nevertheless, President Houphouet-Boigny has said publicly that the Ivory Coast welcomes American investment, trade, and service contracts.

The country's investment laws are among the most liberal in the world. Virtually any foreign firm can qualify to do business in that country simply by registration. However, prior approval is required in a few cases in such fields as processing of local agricultural commodities, finance, and transportation.

Taking 1978 figures, about $100 million of the total direct investments are American. The bulk of these investments are in petroleum distribution, banking, insurance, textiles, chemicals, and household products. Also, in 1978 more than 100 American firms had established regional offices there to market goods and serivces throughout West Africa. To all this, add many millions of dollars in intra-company short-term credits and receivables, and perhaps something around $500-$600 million in medium and long-term bank lending, primarily to the Ivory Coast government.

Between 1976 and 1977, U.S. exports rose from $100.9 million to $142.2 million. The U.S. share of the market is 13.1 percent, taking into account only direct exports from the United States, but this percentage is much higher when we add a greater or equal amount of goods shipped from U.S. owned factories in Europe. When we look at total quantities and total value of U.S.-Ivory Coast trade in agricultural products, again the Ivory Coast came out better than the United States, during the period 1976-77.[7]

7/ See: Table V-3, Source: Agricultural Situation Review, Department of Agriculture, 1977.

Bibliography

Africa and Asia, Agricultural Situation Review. U.S. Department of Agriculture, 1977.

Azikiwe, Nnandi. The Future of Pan-Africanism. London: Nigeria Information Service, 1961.

Balassa, Bela. The Theory of Economic Integration. London: George Allen & Unwin, Ltd., 1965.

Chisiza, D. U. Realities of African Independence. London: The Africa Publications Trust, 1961.

Hargreaves, J. D. Prelude to the Partition of West Africa. London: Macmillan, 1963.

Legum, Colin. Pan-Africanism: A Short Political Guide. New York: Frederick A. Praeger, 1962.

Mutharika, B. W. T. Toward Multinational Economic Cooperation in Africa. New York: Praeger, 1972.

Nkrumah, Kwame. Africa Must Unite. London: Heinemann Educational Books Ltd., 1963.

Nurkse, Ragnar. Problems of Capital Formation in Underdeveloped Countries. Oxford: Basil Blackwell, 1953.

Nyerere, Julius K. Freedom and Unity: A Selection from Writings and Speeches 1952-1965. Dar-es-Salaam: Oxford University Press, 1967.

Overseas Business Report. OBR 77-22, U.S. Department of Commerce, 1977.

Overseas Business Report. OBR 77-28, U.S. Department of Commerce, 1977.

Robinson, E. A. G. Economic Consequences of the Size of Nations. London: Macmillan, 1960.

Thompson, N. and R. Adloff. The Emerging States of French Equatorial Africa. London: Oxford University Press, 1960.

The World Bank. The World Development Report, August 1978. Washington, D.C.

The World Bank. Annual Report. 1978. Washington, D.C.

Table V-1
U.S. TRADE WITH KENYA

1976-1977

Commodity	Quantity		Value	
	1976	1977	1976	1977
	1,000 metric tons		1,000 dollars	
Exports:				
Wheat	0	26.4	0	2,911
Tobacco	0	0.6	0	1,934
Inedible tallow	1.4	1.6	638	736
Vegetable seed	--	--	140	237
Other agricultural	--	--	3,143	1,546
Total agricultural	--	--	3,921	7,364
Total exports	--	--	42,874	76,814
Imports:				
Coffee	13.9	12.7	32,916	54,671
Tea	10.7	9.5	13,828	22,605
Pyrethrum	0.2	0.3	5,377	5,485
Cashew nuts	0.7	0.7	1,491	2,376
Other agricultural	--	--	1,439	1,507
Total agricultural	--	--	55,051	86,644
Total imports	--	--	60,201	92,179

Table V-2
U.S. TRADE WITH TANZANIA

1976-1977

Commodity	Quantity 1976	Quantity 1977	Value 1976	Value 1977
	1,000 metric tons		1,000 dollars	
Exports:				
Sorghum meal and/or cornmeal	30.0	20.0	6,991	4,589
Rice	--	17.9	13	4,408
Corn	42.4	37.3	5,437	4,009
Soybean oil	0	3.0	0	1,483
Other agricultural	--	--	6,677	5,042
Total agricultural	--	--	19,118	19,531
Total exports	--	--	35,690	38,610
Imports:				
Coffee	13.6	13.0	31,023	60,230
Cashew nuts	1.5	1.8	2,758	5,936
Pyrethrum	0.1	0.1	1,571	1,831
Tea	0.5	0.4	643	1,106
Other agricultural	--	--	2,716	4,204
Total agricultural	--	--	38,711	73,307
Total imports	--	--	46,769	78,498

Table V-3
U.S. TRADE WITH IVORY COAST

1976-1977

Commodity	Quantity		Value	
	1976	1977	1976	1977
	1,000 metric tons		1,000 dollars	
Exports:				
Rice	2.4	43.5	1,244	11,862
Tobacco	0.1	0.1	224	468
Grain Sorghum	0	5.0	0	462
Other agricultural	--	--	749	853
Total agricultural	--	--	2,217	13,645
Total exports	--	--	63,303	88,091
Imports:				
Coffee	79.8	40.4	171,643	186,605
Cocoa beans	19.1	38.6	27,375	70,915
Cocoa butter	8.7	6.5	35,324	35,842
Cocoa and cococake	5.7	5.7	5,450	16,457
Other agricultural	--	--	2,662	2,102
Total agricultural	--	--	242,454	311,921
Total imports	--	--	253,439	318,989

Annex VI
ASEAN: Asia's Trade Bloc

George J. Vicksnins

Regional economic cooperation in Southeast Asia dates back to the formation of the Association of Southeast Asia (ASA) in 1961 by the Federation of Malaya, Thailand, and the Philippines. On August 8, 1967, the above three countries were joined by newly-independent Singapore as well as Indonesia in signing the so-called Bangkok Declaration, which established the Association of Southeast Asian Nations. Like its predecessor organization, during much of its first decade, ASEAN emphasized rather casual socioeconomic and technical cooperation -- as Saburo Okita has put it: "...a place where foreign ministers got together to enjoy tea." The political significance of ASEAN appears to have grown quite rapidly since the disengagement of U.S. forces from Indochina; indeed, the first summit meeting between the heads of government took place in Den Pasar, Bali, Indonesia, in February 1976. The Bali Summit produced the first concrete steps toward meaningful regional cooperation: 1) the Treaty of Amity and Cooperation; and, 2) the Declaration of ASEAN Concord. The latter document gave rise to the widely-quoted statement that called for the "...early establishment of a Zone of Peace, Freedom and Neutrality."

The countries of ASEAN have since then moved quite quickly to establish political and economic relations with the Communist countries of Asia, and a rough balance of great-power influence in the region appears to have been achieved. While the recent Vietnamese incursion into Cambodia and China's response remains a threat to stability for the region as a whole, and there exist areas of insurgency activity in nearly every country, the so-called "domino theory" appears to be discredited. This may be partly due to the greater political cohesiveness generated by the activities of the ASEAN organization itself.

At the very least, ASEAN has been successful in avoiding "family feuds" among the five nations themselves and it has presented a united front to the outside world on various political and economic issues. A permanent secretariat was established in 1976, located in Jakarta. Both Taiwan and Sri Lanka have reportedly tried to join the group without success, though Burma will not, despite having been invited. The second summit meeting, at Kuala Lumpur in August 1977, was also attended by the prime ministers of Japan, Australia, and New Zealand. The United States has responded favorably to ASEAN -- in fact, various communist commentators have at times charged that ASEAN is an American-inspired replacement for SEATO. A high-level ASEAN delegation visited Washington in August 1978, and (according to the Far Eastern Economic Review) "...received a firm but generalized commitment from the U.S. administration to the region's overall priorities."

From an economic point of view, ASEAN has a total GNP of about $75 billion and a population base of some 250 million people. These statistics can be somewhat misleading, however, since per capita income averages only around $300, and the vast majority of the population continues to live under conditions of extreme poverty. Singapore, with a population of slightly more than two million, has the highest per capita GNP (nearly $3,000 per year) and has been growing most rapidly. The second-wealthiest country is Malaysia (at about $1,000 per capita), with a population of some 12 million. At the other end of the spectrum is Indonesia's population of about 140 million people, with a per capita GNP somewhat below $300, of whom nearly half are illiterate and malnourished. While GNP growth in all five countries has been rapid in recent years -- in part, due to favorable price trends for petroleum and other raw materials -- the benefits of this growth have not affected the living standards of the poor majority very much.

The countries of ASEAN are quite well-off in terms of natural resources. Except for Java and Singapore, the ratios of land to population are still fairly comfortable -- there exist land reserves that could be brought under cultivation. Water and air pollution has been minimal, and animal life abounds. Both Indonesia and Malaysia have significant amounts of oil and gas, and Thailand is scheduled to start using gas from the finds in the Gulf of Thailand very shortly. The use of geothermal energy is moving ahead in the Philippines very rapidly, and the region

as a whole still has large untapped hydroelectric
resources (the giant Pa Mong project awaits cooperation between Vietnam and Thailand, for example) and
coal deposits. ASEAN exports about 80 percent of the
world's natural rubber, palm oil, and tin, and there
exist significant deposits of chrome, copper, nickel,
bauxite, and gold. Perhaps even more important than
known resource supplies is the region's potential,
for much of the region remains unexplored.

ASEAN as a trade bloc has gotten its start only
recently. While the countries of the region have all
followed a strategy of "export-led growth" to some
extent, the bulk of their trade has been with more
developed countries, notably Japan and the United
States. Quantitatively, ASEAN's trade with Japan has
been some 24.5 percent of its total foreign trade
(in 1977), while Japan's trade with the ASEAN bloc
was 9.9 percent of its total. For the United States,
the picture is much the same -- for ASEAN, the United
States accounts for 18 percent of the total, while
for the United States the ASEAN countries constitute
only 4 percent of trade. In terms of recent trends,
Japan's exports to the region have been growing more
rapidly than those from the United States -- for
example, Thailand's imports from the United States
have declined from 17 percent of the total in 1960
to 13 percent in 1976, while Japanese sales have
risen from 26 percent to 32 percent over the same
period.

U.S. direct investment in the ASEAN countries,
while growing quite rapidly, remains relatively
insignificant in global terms. According to the
latest Department of Commerce estimates, the total
for all of Asia, except Japan, was slightly above
$6 billion, or about 4 percent of the total U.S.
foreign investment position. The U.S. investment
total for Indonesia is the largest individual item,
adding up to $1,138 million at the end of 1977; of
this, the bulk was in the petroleum industry, with
only $105 million in manufacturing. The next largest
recipient of U.S. direct investment was the Philippines,
with accumulative total of $913 million. In this case,
investments in the manufacturing sector are considerably
more important -- at about 40 percent of the total,
with a large number of firms located in the Bataan
export processing zone. Thirdly, the United States is
still the largest foreign investor in Singapore, with
a total estimated at more than $500 million, but Japan
is moving ahead very rapidly. Malaysia's policy of
emphasizing indigenous Malay control of investment
projects has caused considerable disinvestment to

take place over the last three years, with the U.S.
investment position currently valued at around $200
million. The total is somewhat smaller in Thailand
although the natural gas finds by Union and Texas
Pacific plus the decision to develop the port at
Sattahip into an industrial estate should attract
new U.S. funds.

Trade liberalization among the ASEAN countries
themselves has been proceeding rather slowly. In
general, relatively little complementarity exists
among the five economies; rather, there is a competitive relationship in a number of specific
commodities (tin, rubber, timber, textiles, etc.).
In 1977, four primary products accounted for slightly
more than 80 percent of Indonesia's exports (petroleum
alone was 67.2 percent). Malaysia's exports of five
products (rubber, tin, wood, petroleum, and palm oil)
have fluctuated between 70 percent and 80 percent of
its total trade in every year since 1970, despite a
rapidly expanding manufacturing sector. For the
Philippines, four products still account for 55 percent of the total -- though the concentration ratio
has fallen (from 78.7 percent in 1970). The same
reliance on primary products exists in Thailand, where
six items account for some 60 percent of total
earnings. As a result of this lack of complementarity,
intra-ASEAN trade accounts for only about 15 percent
of their total exports, and a large part of that
total can be attributed to raw material purchases
from neighboring sources by industrial Singapore. In
1977, Singapore announced bilateral agreements with
both the Philippines and Thailand, which involved a
10 percent across-the-board tariff reduction for more
than 1,750 commodities. Following this lead, the
Kuala Lumpur Summit Meeting cut tariffs on 71 commodity items, involving about $150 million in trade
turnover, effective January 1, 1978. At the ASEAN
economic minister's meeting, an additional 755 items
were approved for inclusion in the preferential tariff
arrangement of about a 10 percent cut. The ministers
also agreed that, at each subsequent round of negotia-
tion, each member country would offer to add an
additional 100 items to the liberalization list. The
commodity-by-commodity approach adopted by the ASEAN
countries thus far is probably more restrictive than
an overall tariff reduction scheme -- involving, say,
a 20 percent - 25 percent preference for all ASEAN-
produced items -- but these have been positive steps
in the direction of a customs union.

In addition to these trade liberalization
measures, ASEAN is also attempting a regional

approach to industrial development. Theoretically,
this concept has a great deal of appeal -- since each
nation's domestic market for industrial products is
rather small, due to population size or income levels
or both, integrated industrial development along
regional lines should be able to realize considerable
economies of scale. Thus, the Bali Summit developed
a "package deal" program whereby each nation would
pursue one big industrial project for the whole ASEAN
market. It was proposed to construct a diesel engine
plant in Singapore, a soda-ash factory in Thailand, a
superphosphate plant in the Philippines, and one urea
plant in Malaysia and another in Indonesia. The investment costs were covered by 75 percent foreign
credit, but the remainder by local equity capital --
with 60 percent of the latter amount coming from the
country in which the project is located and the other
40 percent from the other four ASEAN countries.
Project implementation has been very slow, however,
despite Japan's repeated promises to help with the
foreign exchange costs. Indonesia is already producing diesel engines of up to 500 horse power, and
has asked Singapore to limit itself to larger ones
(for which there is only a limited regional market);
the Philippines lacks raw materials for its project,
and Thailand has had serious misgivings about the
plant's location. (For further details, see Rolf
Hanisch, "ASEAN: The Long Road to Regional Cooperation," Inter-economics, Jan./Feb. 1978.)   Others
have criticized the decision to concentrate on
industrial projects, arguing that it is much more
significant for ASEAN countries to focus on a rural-
based development strategy.
     In addition to trade liberalization and an
approach to industrial integration, a number of other
ASEAN initiatives can be cited. The Kuala Lumpur
Summit agreed to give ASEAN countries "mutual preferences with respect to the purchase and sales of
basic commodities" (such as rice or oil) under
emergency conditions. Various private groups, such
as Chambers of Commerce and bankers, have been meeting
regularly and developing institutional arrangements
for regional cooperation, e.g., training bank personnel. The governors of ASEAN central banks have set
up a $100 million Swap Arrangement, which enables a
member central bank to draw up to $40 million at a
time (though at commercial rates). In general, however, the significance of ASEAN as a economic entity
has probably lagged behind its political development.
Its diplomatic accomplishments have been quite
impressive, and it has been very effective in making

130

its case in bilateral negotiations as well as in
multilateral agencies. We can conclude this assess-
ment of ASEAN by quoting the Honorable S. Rajaratnam:

> ...Far more than people realize, ASEAN has
> succeeded in compelling its members to balance
> national interests with the imperatives of
> collective interests. ASEAN solidarity is both
> directed and institutionalized. Many routine
> problems which before ASEAN would have been
> discussed and disposed of in purely national
> terms are now increasingly discussed and
> resolved in ASEAN terms.

(Cf. L. R. Vasey and G. J. Viksnins (eds.), The Economic
and Political Growth Pattern of Asia-Pacific (Honolulu:
University of Hawaii Press, 1976), p. 16.)

Selected Bibliography

For general background, see the proceedings of two
recent conferences organized by the Pacific Forum:
L. R. Vasey and G. J. Viksnins (eds.), The Economic
and Political Growth Pattern of Asia-Pacific (Honolulu:
University of Hawaii Press for the Pacific Forum,
1978). For economic assessments, see W. S. Hundsberger,
W. K. Chan, and C. E. Meleky, "Economic Cooperation/
Integration in the ASPAC and ASEAN Area," Asia
Quarterly, 1974/2, and Rolf Hanisch, "ASEAN: The
Long Road to Regional Cooperation," Inter-economics,
Jan./Feb. 1978. For further documentation on recent
trade preference negotiations, see Jap Kim Siong,
"ASEAN: Recent Development in Trade Preferences and
Comprehensive Double Taxation Agreements," Inter-
national Bulletin of Fiscal Documentation, February
1978. A recent discussion of political issues will
be found in Alejandro Melchor, Jr., "Assessing
ASEAN's Viability in a Changing World," Asian Survey,
April 1978.

Annex VII
Statistical Survey

Note: Membership in each trading bloc for the entire
       time period is held constant at its 1978 com-
       position.

       See caveats on data coverage and quality in
       Explanatory Notes to Annex III.

Tables VII 1-13

Exports and Imports of Trading Blocs, with
U.S., Bloc and World, by Bloc, 1950-1977,
millions of dollars.

Note: Data for 1977 are in many cases
Incomplete and preliminary.

Source: IMF files.

Table VII-1
AFRICAN AND MAURITIAN COMMON ORGANIZATION (OCAM):

INTERNATIONAL TRADE 1950-1977
(Millions of dollars)

	EXPORTS TO:			IMPORTS FROM:		
Year	United States	World	OCAM	United States	World	OCAM
1950	35	271	0	48	191	0
1951	39	450	0	69	348	0
1952	52	456	0	100	449	0
1953	68	467	0	84	413	0
1954	67	465	0	70	416	0
1955	78	521	0	73	431	0
1956	78	611	0	84	463	0
1957	65	555	0	78	494	0
1958	95	499	0	47	398	0
1959	109	574	0	38	355	0
1960	95	966	7	52	789	11
1961	87	987	9	58	870	16
1962	88	951	17	104	925	23
1963	110	1,018	18	118	947	33
1964	132	1,146	28	121	1,136	35
1965	109	1,117	38	120	1,179	36
1966	116	1,320	41	124	1,230	40
1967	111	1,323	55	92	1,220	57
1968	132	1,518	61	106	1,304	58
1969	118	1,723	55	125	1,553	49
1970	141	1,834	65	133	1,686	54
1971	166	1,715	85	175	1,911	55
1972	149	2,154	109	152	2,325	90
1973	189	2,910	144	205	2,929	107
1974	373	4,783	207	290	4,008	148
1975	528	4,541	248	438	4,771	241
1976	700	5,312	199	351	4,782	201
1977	811	6,360	4	405	5,833	5

Table VII-2
ANDEAN SUBREGIONAL GROUP (ANCOM):

INTERNATIONAL TRADE 1950-1977
(Millions of dollars)

Year	EXPORTS TO:			IMPORTS FROM:		
	United States	World	ANCOM	United States	World	ANCOM
1950	955	2,209	65	933	1,485	57
1951	1,166	2,639	51	1,168	1,881	54
1952	1,344	2,852	75	1,289	2,065	58
1953	1,481	2,868	68	1,348	2,213	58
1954	1,544	3,195	60	1,385	2,417	60
1955	1,557	3,394	77	1,455	2,599	61
1956	1,742	3,774	74	1,499	2,674	58
1957	1,746	3,862	78	1,972	3,344	67
1958	1,640	3,654	54	1,597	2,886	42
1959	1,689	3,848	75	1,503	2,829	53
1960	1,815	4,060	62	1,388	2,738	59
1961	1,648	4,021	55	1,399	2,874	67
1962	1,642	4,316	69	1,343	2,879	73
1963	1,594	4,373	68	1,313	2,894	91
1964	1,745	4,827	90	1,543	3,304	95
1965	1,789	4,941	100	1,606	3,540	117
1966	1,897	5,154	130	1,751	3,898	141
1967	1,835	5,396	119	1,659	3,886	159
1968	1,850	5,587	148	1,864	4,139	141
1969	1,816	5,796	153	1,847	4,330	178
1970	2,160	6,661	150	2,064	4,780	186
1971	1,952	6,025	203	1,972	5,162	236
1972	2,162	6,293	218	1,952	5,466	225
1973	2,980	8,490	304	2,267	6,572	278
1974	6,701	17,385	609	3,870	10,283	574
1975	5,129	14,165	771	4,827	12,301	828
1976	5,123	15,229	752	5,207	13,444	804
1977	5,978	13,835	528	6,175	17,359	591

Table VII-3

ASSOCIATION OF SOUTH-EAST ASIAN NATIONS (ASEAN):

INTERNATIONAL TRADE 1950-1977
(Millions of dollars)

Year	EXPORTS TO:			IMPORTS FROM:		
	United States	World	ASEAN	United States	World	ASEAN
1950	454	1,348	22	398	979	24
1951	609	2,022	59	624	1,655	67
1952	573	1,566	65	599	1,731	76
1953	519	1,474	30	653	1,627	36
1954	449	1,463	34	553	1,482	40
1955	512	1,604	40	567	1,548	50
1956	467	1,667	51	529	1,780	67
1957	447	1,767	70	572	1,887	83
1958	536	1,567	148	513	1,898	165
1959	601	1,648	143	450	1,855	157
1960	560	1,711	132	534	2,172	145
1961	485	1,738	338	528	1,981	191
1962	429	1,853	304	547	2,416	219
1963	461	2,034	246	503	2,403	175
1964	561	2,055	98	468	2,150	119
1965	542	2,097	54	492	2,321	111
1966	711	3,434	230	626	3,971	274
1967	736	3,742	703	774	5,107	742
1968	900	4,870	1,031	941	5,935	793
1969	989	5,579	1,198	936	6,479	886
1970	1,064	6,094	1,166	1,113	7,350	921
1971	1,170	6,569	1,270	1,145	7,968	961
1972	1,411	7,822	1,396	1,448	9,375	1,149
1973	2,256	13,348	2,245	2,273	14,167	1,677
1974	4,365	22,591	3,282	3,434	22,946	2,441
1975	4,131	20,763	3,262	3,614	23,322	2,356
1976	5,468	25,984	3,740	4,031	26,230	3,263
1977	6,849	31,817	4,592	4,114	30,137	3,746

Table VII-4
CARIBBEAN COMMON MARKET (CARICOM):

INTERNATIONAL TRADE 1950-1977
(Millions of dollars)

Year	EXPORTS TO:			IMPORTS FROM:		
	United States	World	CARICOM	United States	World	CARICOM
1950	10	144	0	17	157	2
1951	13	202	2	33	247	2
1952	13	229	6	42	287	6
1953	20	266	6	32	274	7
1954	24	288	7	36	296	7
1955	25	312	13	50	356	14
1956	36	358	13	69	397	13
1957	54	432	16	84	464	15
1958	94	446	20	92	543	18
1959	84	483	16	94	568	24
1960	113	551	22	122	664	29
1961	168	639	22	122	703	27
1962	180	660	32	140	742	30
1963	190	731	29	158	747	28
1964	213	765	27	186	874	33
1965	237	761	30	216	965	33
1966	277	829	38	231	998	33
1967	311	831	43	259	996	36
1968	340	837	41	263	1,016	35
1969	383	907	51	312	1,147	46
1970	472	1,021	46	391	1,375	39
1971	443	1,087	82	406	1,529	70
1972	474	1,142	92	451	1,711	97
1973	603	1,308	120	479	1,843	119
1974	1,831	3,172	197	660	3,305	208
1975	1,656	3,096	230	920	3,232	246
1976	1,888	3,224	230	916	3,590	247
1977	2,005	3,198	189	857	2,991	205

138

Table VII-5
CENTRAL AMERICAN COMMON MARKET (CACM):

INTERNATIONAL TRADE 1950-1977
(Millions of dollars)

	EXPORTS TO:			IMPORTS FROM:		
Year	United States	World	CACM	United States	World	CACM
1950	203	245	8	161	223	7
1951	240	301	10	193	278	9
1952	274	359	10	211	313	10
1953	271	377	11	213	327	11
1954	266	405	14	234	373	14
1955	250	513	13	259	415	13
1956	241	432	15	282	463	14
1957	248	466	18	299	520	17
1958	228	451	21	275	498	21
1959	199	434	29	237	466	28
1960	216	444	31	250	514	33
1961	222	446	37	230	495	37
1962	234	500	40	254	552	48
1963	248	586	69	289	647	67
1964	246	677	105	335	770	107
1965	283	762	133	364	891	136
1966	299	846	172	385	937	176
1967	296	855	205	411	1,030	213
1968	311	951	248	400	1,040	253
1969	344	980	253	380	1,065	249
1970	379	1,105	287	438	1,234	299
1971	419	1,136	276	444	1,305	277
1972	446	1,358	308	458	1,387	305
1973	613	1,667	385	624	1,846	388
1974	648	2,116	534	978	2,924	526
1975	751	2,309	541	1,018	2,946	519
1976	1,130	3,012	653	1,140	3,310	611
1977	1,377	3,618	264	1,561	3,589	288

Table VII-6
COUNCIL OF THE ENTENTE STATES TRADE

INTERNATIONAL TRADE 1950-1977
(Millions of dollars)

Year	EXPORTS TO:			IMPORTS FROM:		
	United States	World	Council of the Entente States	United States	World	Council of the Entente States
1950	0	0	0	0	0	0
1951	0	0	0	0	0	0
1952	0	0	0	0	0	0
1953	0	0	0	0	0	0
1954	0	0	0	0	0	0
1955	0	0	0	0	0	0
1956	0	0	0	0	0	0
1957	0	0	0	0	0	0
1958	0	14	0	0	11	0
1959	2	17	0	0	15	0
1960	24	201	2	6	198	3
1961	28	229	2	8	254	5
1962	30	242	4	11	269	5
1963	33	289	5	11	291	11
1964	63	378	10	27	389	12
1965	44	357	14	17	389	12
1966	55	408	17	26	421	14
1967	47	429	21	24	440	15
1968	69	533	23	27	489	16
1969	67	581	20	39	553	18
1970	89	607	19	43	623	17
1971	79	608	18	39	653	18
1972	77	700	28	43	751	22
1973	98	1,054	44	82	1,087	25
1974	87	1,524	64	100	1,483	37
1975	126	1,496	83	127	1,755	46
1976	173	1,970	71	140	2,008	47
1977	298	2,620	0	161	2,416	0

Table VII-7
EAST AFRICAN COMMON MARKET (EACM):

INTERNATIONAL TRADE 1950-1977
(Millions of dollars)

	EXPORTS TO:			IMPORTS FROM:		
Year	United States	World	EACM	United States	World	EACM
1950	20	202	0	11	201	0
1951	34	316	0	9	282	0
1952	38	344	0	16	334	0
1953	25	253	0	15	289	0
1954	27	283	0	10	325	0
1955	35	302	0	14	414	0
1956	33	337	0	11	371	0
1957	42	332	0	10	390	0
1958	42	342	0	10	339	0
1959	35	360	0	11	339	0
1960	43	391	0	18	375	0
1961	43	373	0	20	378	0
1962	51	388	0	26	380	0
1963	60	478	0	19	407	0
1964	81	535	0	25	428	0
1965	58	504	0	37	503	0
1966	80	599	0	47	615	0
1967	61	573	0	43	597	0
1968	75	708	119	39	775	119
1969	79	744	118	41	774	116
1970	92	845	142	64	934	142
1971	87	859	151	74	1,198	149
1972	91	964	130	58	1,105	126
1973	109	1,125	151	65	1,267	151
1974	127	1,350	172	119	2,052	172
1975	111	1,268	159	173	1,978	155
1976	211	1,646	192	102	1,789	192
1977	368	2,140	154	114	2,231	161

Table VII-8
EUROPEAN ECONOMIC COMMUNITY (EEC):

INTERNATIONAL TRADE 1950-1977
(Millions of dollars)

Year	EXPORTS TO:			IMPORTS FROM:		
	United States	World	EEC	United States	World	EEC
1950	881	16,474	5,814	2,430	19,849	5,905
1951	1,387	22,422	7,400	3,558	27,702	7,344
1952	1,419	22,560	7,272	3,217	26,387	7,331
1953	1,562	22,810	7,745	2,390	25,823	7,691
1954	1,444	24,840	8,594	2,694	27,774	8,549
1955	1,792	28,199	10,014	3,696	31,937	9,976
1956	2,212	30,758	10,987	4,399	35,071	11,023
1957	2,327	33,733	11,930	5,354	38,205	11,899
1958	2,649	33,783	11,626	3,970	35,546	11,720
1959	3,706	36,903	13,421	3,907	38,006	13,493
1960	3,461	42,269	16,186	5,660	45,141	16,249
1961	3,351	45,450	18,386	5,651	47,590	18,262
1962	3,710	45,736	20,567	6,066	51,756	20,620
1963	3,892	52,231	23,567	6,690	57,376	23,613
1964	4,256	58,050	26,826	7,534	64,510	26,978
1965	5,090	64,585	29,599	7,875	69,140	29,746
1966	6,179	70,462	32,458	8,359	74,533	32,841
1967	6,433	73,859	34,113	8,441	77,149	34,467
1968	8,243	83,021	39,202	9,362	85,578	39,456
1969	8,485	97,611	48,225	10,460	101,258	48,675
1970	9,269	112,594	56,411	12,303	116,529	56,877
1971	10,830	129,115	65,225	12,244	130,641	65,940
1972	12,698	155,382	80,634	12,906	155,056	80,826
1973	15,794	212,302	111,226	18,054	217,186	111,766
1974	19,029	276,742	139,353	23,699	295,873	140,381
1975	16,399	298,164	146,340	24,766	301,583	147,964
1976	18,162	328,182	168,905	27,409	344,694	169,053
1977	22,807	381,662	192,824	28,943	388,996	192,480

Table VII-9
EUROPEAN FREE TRADE ASSOCIATION (EFTA):

INTERNATIONAL TRADE 1950-1977
(Millions of dollars)

Year	EXPORTS TO:			IMPORTS FROM:		
	United States	World	EFTA	United States	World	EFTA
1950	304	3,283	313	502	4,011	317
1951	402	5,074	465	741	5,711	480
1952	405	4,712	481	699	5,639	504
1953	471	4,541	423	499	5,123	434
1954	376	4,976	507	526	5,826	517
1955	410	5,488	564	677	6,706	586
1956	473	6,144	628	828	7,577	649
1957	446	6,684	714	963	8,282	729
1958	456	6,414	703	733	7,749	701
1959	595	6,864	759	717	8,191	760
1960	558	7,836	942	958	9,689	946
1961	545	8,375	1,089	945	10,604	1,099
1962	650	8,942	1,192	944	11,244	1,222
1963	682	9,682	1,328	974	12,104	1,332
1964	768	10,986	1,587	1,133	13,708	1,579
1965	894	12,127	1,839	1,172	15,093	1,852
1966	1,060	13,072	2,049	1,264	16,149	2,049
1967	1,093	13,892	2,301	1,211	16,746	2,317
1968	1,251	15,316	2,454	1,323	17,591	2,456
1969	1,294	17,862	3,013	1,443	20,346	3,025
1970	1,364	20,656	3,831	1,807	25,109	3,880
1971	1,564	22,484	4,267	1,751	27,346	4,317
1972	1,974	27,211	5,158	1,959	31,743	5,112
1973	2,429	37,640	6,939	2,543	43,344	6,943
1974	2,799	49,412	9,522	3,774	60,361	9,330
1975	2,755	52,782	9,876	4,107	62,349	9,956
1976	2,886	58,279	10,273	4,183	68,664	10,479
1977	3,488	65,360	11,318	4,760	78,259	11,217

Table VII-10
LATIN AMERICAN FREE TRADE ASSOCIATION (LAFTA):

INTERNATIONAL TRADE 1950-1977
(Millions of dollars)

	EXPORTS TO:			IMPORTS FROM:		
Year	United States	World	LAFTA	United States	World	LAFTA
1950	2,335	5,100	356	1,905	3,890	374
1951	2,698	6,183	485	2,917	5,930	539
1952	2,708	5,589	441	2,975	6,032	554
1953	2,781	6,099	584	2,516	5,187	648
1954	2,617	6,368	537	2,717	5,806	601
1955	2,746	6,403	588	2,623	5,967	674
1956	3,082	6,897	488	2,926	6,101	549
1957	2,979	6,847	553	3,725	7,261	671
1958	2,750	6,660	541	3,162	6,635	640
1959	2,839	6,919	514	2,895	6,229	590
1960	2,933	7,200	509	3,024	6,673	590
1961	2,804	6,245	447	3,101	6,973	533
1962	2,778	7,711	503	2,993	6,892	585
1963	2,885	8,156	530	2,872	6,638	660
1964	2,935	8,772	675	3,266	7,176	764
1965	3,025	9,228	778	3,241	7,447	913
1966	3,266	9,761	793	3,634	8,183	898
1967	3,139	9,707	783	3,589	8,470	933
1968	3,359	10,135	927	4,017	9,473	1,009
1969	3,388	11,198	1,072	4,193	10,328	1,211
1970	3,752	12,550	1,148	4,852	11,715	1,239
1971	3,691	12,131	1,270	4,798	13,064	1,344
1972	4,419	14,019	1,525	5,252	14,951	1,540
1973	5,706	20,347	2,204	7,048	19,742	2,140
1974	10,495	32,432	3,571	11,717	34,333	3,625
1975	8,344	28,888	3,686	12,995	36,630	3,760
1976	9,387	32,991	4,015	12,656	36,471	4,205
1977	10,990	36,069	4,579	13,105	40,481	4,853

Table VII-11
MAGHREB GROUP

INTERNATIONAL TRADE 1950-1977
(Millions of dollars)

	EXPORTS TO:			IMPORTS FROM:		
Year	United States	World	Maghreb Group	United States	World	Maghreb Group
1950	11	630	28	53	904	24
1951	14	738	35	73	1,214	29
1952	18	797	38	85	1,334	33
1953	18	773	42	64	1,234	38
1954	19	814	42	73	1,269	41
1955	20	897	39	70	1,373	37
1956	11	880	40	86	1,417	39
1957	14	944	37	110	1,638	38
1958	12	986	40	77	1,691	39
1959	13	840	37	63	1,627	37
1960	11	866	37	70	1,864	14
1961	11	817	30	115	1,672	30
1962	17	1,201	23	150	1,431	26
1963	7	1,176	22	119	1,431	24
1964	12	1,286	21	94	1,414	30
1965	14	1,186	24	110	1,369	26
1966	14	1,191	14	159	1,368	17
1967	15	1,296	15	170	1,414	14
1968	16	1,432	19	187	1,577	19
1969	13	1,585	32	180	1,814	35
1970	18	1,662	37	230	2,218	39
1971	26	1,544	35	251	2,240	39
1972	131	2,237	49	217	2,707	52
1973	282	3,234	76	369	4,078	77
1974	1,162	7,316	136	772	7,292	136
1975	1,393	7,098	76	1,197	9,990	58
1976	2,472	7,383	35	951	9,473	38
1977	3,150	7,615	34	951	11,583	35

Table VII-12
UNION OF CENTRAL AFRICAN STATES (UDEAC):

INTERNATIONAL TRADE 1950-1977
(Millions of dollars)

Year	EXPORTS TO:			IMPORTS FROM:		
	United States	World	UDEAC	United States	World	UDEAC
1950	1	46	0	6	60	0
1951	3	64	0	6	93	0
1952	4	62	0	10	106	0
1953	7	74	0	4	80	0
1954	9	87	0	5	93	0
1955	10	95	0	7	104	0
1956	6	75	0	7	95	0
1957	5	85	0	5	100	0
1958	6	106	0	6	102	0
1959	11	108	0	4	81	0
1960	8	176	2	13	206	1
1961	7	186	2	15	240	1
1962	12	209	1	13	234	1
1963	20	255	3	16	244	2
1964	30	296	3	17	266	2
1965	39	296	4	21	289	3
1966	47	306	2	18	301	2
1967	50	323	1	19	371	3
1968	47	395	10	23	363	9
1969	34	455	12	28	400	11
1970	27	416	12	33	412	13
1971	34	456	13	36	453	13
1972	44	537	22	55	574	19
1973	55	780	21	57	671	17
1974	226	1,519	21	60	939	33
1975	296	1,616	30	68	1,304	50
1976	284	1,889	39	88	1,342	44
1977	295	2,008	67	86	1,756	57

Table VII-13
WEST AFRICAN ECONOMIC COMMUNITY (CEAO):

INTERNATIONAL TRADE 1950-1977
(Millions of dollars)

	EXPORTS TO:			IMPORTS FROM:		
Year	United States	World	CEAO	United States	World	CEAO
1950	0	0	0	0	0	0
1951	0	0	0	0	0	0
1952	0	0	0	0	0	0
1953	0	0	0	0	0	0
1954	0	0	0	0	0	0
1955	0	0	0	0	0	0
1956	0	0	0	0	0	0
1957	0	0	0	0	0	0
1958	0	0	0	0	0	0
1959	0	0	0	0	0	0
1960	23	306	2	11	372	5
1961	26	350	6	14	452	12
1962	28	362	13	20	477	19
1963	32	408	14	23	494	27
1964	62	532	22	38	571	26
1965	45	531	34	29	574	28
1966	55	604	33	37	689	30
1967	47	626	43	36	652	42
1968	69	730	49	37	589	44
1969	67	756	41	56	785	35
1970	90	829	52	58	848	42
1971	79	803	73	62	921	43
1972	78	1,015	101	65	1,094	73
1973	97	1,393	136	126	1,589	91
1974	89	1,973	183	163	2,160	116
1975	127	2,053	222	184	2,574	195
1976	176	2,321	156	195	2,684	142
1977	300	3,178	0	203	3,121	0

Tables VII 14-26

Exports and Imports of Trading Blocs, with
U.S., Bloc and World, by Bloc, 1950-1977,
percent.

Note: Data for 1977 are in many cases incomplete
and preliminary.

Source: IMF files.

Table VII-14

AFRICAN AND MAURITIAN COMMON ORGANIZATION (COAM):

INTERNATIONAL TRADE 1950-1977
(Percent)

| Year | EXPORTS TO: | | IMPORTS FROM: |
	U.S. as % of Total Exports	OCAM as % of Total Exports	U.S. as % of Total Imports
1950	13	0	25
1951	9	0	20
1952	11	0	22
1953	15	0	20
1954	14	0	17
1955	15	0	17
1956	13	0	18
1957	12	0	16
1958	19	0	12
1959	19	0	11
1960	10	1	7
1961	9	1	7
1962	10	2	11
1963	11	2	12
1964	12	2	11
1965	10	3	10
1966	9	3	10
1967	8	4	8
1968	9	4	8
1969	7	3	8
1970	8	4	8
1971	10	5	9
1972	7	5	7
1973	6	5	7
1974	8	4	7
1975	12	5	9
1976	13	4	7
1977	13	5	7

Table VII-15
ANDEAN SUBREGIONAL GROUP (ANCOM):

INTERNATIONAL TRADE 1950-1977
(Percent)

	EXPORTS TO:		IMPORTS FROM:
Year	U.S. as % of Total Exports	ANCOM as % of Total Exports	U.S. as % of Total Imports
1950	43	3	63
1951	44	2	62
1952	48	3	62
1953	51	2	61
1954	48	2	57
1955	53	2	56
1956	46	2	56
1957	45	2	59
1958	45	1	55
1959	44	2	53
1960	45	2	51
1961	41	1	49
1962	38	2	47
1963	36	2	45
1964	36	2	47
1965	36	2	45
1966	37	3	45
1967	34	2	43
1968	33	3	45
1969	31	3	43
1970	32	2	43
1971	32	3	38
1972	34	3	36
1973	35	4	34
1974	39	4	38
1975	36	5	39
1976	34	5	39
1977	43	4	36

Table VII-16
ASSOCIATION OF SOUTH-EAST ASIAN NATIONS (ASEAN):

INTERNATIONAL TRADE 1950-1977
(Percent)

| Year | EXPORTS TO: | | IMPORTS FROM: |
	U.S. as % of Total Exports	ASEAN as % of Total Exports	U.S. as % of Total Imports
1950	34	2	41
1951	30	3	38
1952	37	4	35
1953	35	2	40
1954	31	2	37
1955	32	2	37
1956	28	3	30
1957	25	4	30
1958	34	9	27
1959	36	9	24
1960	33	8	25
1961	28	19	27
1962	23	16	23
1963	23	12	21
1964	27	5	22
1965	26	3	21
1966	21	7	16
1967	20	19	15
1968	18	21	16
1969	18	21	14
1970	17	19	15
1971	18	19	14
1972	18	18	15
1973	17	17	16
1974	19	15	15
1975	20	16	15
1976	21	14	15
1977	22	14	14

Table VII-17
CARIBBEAN COMMON MARKET (CARICOM):

INTERNATIONAL TRADE 1950-1977
(Percent)

	EXPORTS TO:		IMPORTS FROM:
Year	U.S. as % of Total Exports	CARICOM as % of Total Exports	U.S. as % of Total Imports
1950	6.9	0	11
1951	6.4	1	13
1952	5.6	2.6	15
1953	7.5	2.3	12
1954	8.3	2.4	12
1955	8.0	4.2	14
1956	10	3.6	17
1957	13	3.7	18
1958	21	4.5	17
1959	17	3.3	17
1960	21	4.0	18
1961	26	3.4	17
1962	27	4.8	19
1963	26	4.0	21
1964	28	3.5	21
1965	31	3.9	22
1966	33	4.0	23
1967	37	5.2	26
1968	41	4.9	26
1969	42	5.6	27
1970	46	4.5	28
1971	41	7.5	27
1972	42	8.1	26
1973	46	9.1	26
1974	58	6.2	20
1975	53	7.4	28
1976	59	7.1	26
1977	63	5.9	29

Table VII-18
CENTRAL AMERICAN COMMON MARKET (CACM):

INTERNATIONAL TRADE 1950-1977
(Percent)

	EXPORTS TO:		IMPORTS FROM:
Year	U.S. as % of Total Exports	CACM as % of Total Exports	U.S. as % of Total Imports
1950	83	3	72
1951	80	3	69
1952	76	3	67
1953	72	3	65
1954	66	3	63
1955	61	3	62
1956	56	3	61
1957	53	4	58
1958	51	5	55
1959	46	7	51
1960	49	7	49
1961	50	8	46
1962	47	8	46
1963	42	12	45
1964	36	16	44
1965	37	17	41
1966	35	20	41
1967	35	24	40
1968	33	26	38
1969	35	26	36
1970	34	26	35
1971	37	24	34
1972	33	23	33
1973	37	23	34
1974	31	25	33
1975	33	23	35
1976	38	22	34
1977	38	7	43

Table VII-19
COUNCIL OF THE ENTENTE STATES

INTERNATIONAL TRADE 1950-1977
(Percent)

Year	EXPORTS TO: U.S. as % of Total Exports	Council on the Entente States as % of Total Exports	IMPORTS FROM: U.S. as % of Total Imports
1950	0	0	0
1951	0	0	0
1952	0	0	0
1953	0	0	0
1954	0	0	0
1955	0	0	0
1956	0	0	0
1957	0	0	0
1958	0	0	0
1959	12	0	0
1960	12	1	3
1961	12	1	3
1962	12	2	4
1963	11	2	4
1964	17	3	7
1965	12	4	4
1966	13	4	6
1967	11	5	5
1968	13	4	5
1969	11	3	7
1970	15	3	7
1971	13	3	6
1972	11	4	6
1973	9	4	7
1974	6	4	7
1975	8	5	7
1976	9	4	7
1977	11	0	7

Table VII-20
EAST AFRICAN COMMON MARKET (EACM):

INTERNATIONAL TRADE 1950-1977
(Percent)

Year	EXPORTS TO:		IMPORTS FROM:
	U.S. as % of Total Exports	EACM as % of Total Exports	U.S. as % of Total Imports
1950	10	0	5
1951	11	0	3
1952	11	0	5
1953	10	0	5
1954	10	0	3
1955	12	0	3
1956	10	0	3
1957	13	0	3
1958	12	0	3
1959	10	0	3
1960	11	0	5
1961	11	0	5
1962	13	0	7
1963	13	0	5
1964	15	0	6
1965	11	0	7
1966	13	0	8
1967	11	0	7
1968	11	17	5
1969	11	16	5
1970	11	17	7
1971	10	18	6
1972	9	13	5
1973	10	13	5
1974	9	13	7
1975	9	12	9
1976	13	12	6
1977	17	7	5

Table VII-21
EUROPEAN ECONOMIC COMMUNITY (EEC):

INTERNATIONAL TRADE 1950-1977
(Percent)

Year	EXPORTS TO:		IMPORTS FROM:	
	U.S. % of Total	EEC % of Total	U.S. % of Total	EEC % of Total
1950	5	35	12	30
1951	6	33	13	26
1952	6	32	12	28
1953	7	34	9	30
1954	6	35	10	31
1955	6	35	12	31
1956	7	36	12	31
1957	7	35	14	31
1958	8	34	11	33
1959	10	36	10	35
1960	8	38	12	36
1961	7	40	12	38
1962	8	43	12	40
1963	7	45	12	41
1964	7	46	12	42
1965	8	46	11	43
1966	9	46	11	44
1967	9	46	11	45
1968	10	47	11	46
1969	9	49	10	48
1970	8	50	11	49
1971	8	50	9	50
1972	8	52	8	52
1973	7	52	8	51
1974	7	50	8	47
1975	5	49	8	49
1976	5	51	8	49
1977	6	50	7	49

Table VII-22
EUROPEAN FREE TRADE ASSOCIATION (EFTA):

INTERNATIONAL TRADE 1950-1977
(Percent)

	EXPORTS TO:		IMPORTS FROM:	
Year	U.S. % of Total	EFTA % of Total	U.S. % of Total	EFTA % of Total
1950	9	9	12	8
1951	8	9	13	8
1952	9	10	12	9
1953	10	9	10	8
1954	8	10	9	9
1955	7	10	10	9
1956	8	10	11	9
1957	7	11	12	9
1958	7	11	9	9
1959	9	11	9	9
1960	7	12	10	10
1961	6	13	9	10
1962	7	13	8	11
1963	7	14	8	11
1964	7	14	8	11
1965	7	15	8	12
1966	8	16	8	13
1967	8	17	7	14
1968	8	16	7	14
1969	7	17	7	15
1970	7	19	7	15
1971	7	19	6	16
1972	7	19	6	16
1973	6	18	6	16
1974	6	19	6	15
1975	5	19	7	16
1976	5	18	6	15
1977	5	17	6	14

Table VII-23
LATIN AMERICAN FREE TRADE ASSOCIATION (LAFTA):

INTERNATIONAL TRADE 1950-1977
(Percent)

Year	EXPORTS TO:		IMPORTS FROM:
	U.S. as % of Total Exports	LAFTA as % of Total Exports	U.S. as % of Total Imports
1950	46	7	49
1951	44	8	49
1952	48	8	49
1953	46	10	49
1954	41	8	47
1955	43	9	44
1956	45	7	48
1957	44	8	51
1958	41	8	48
1959	41	7	46
1960	41	7	45
1961	39	6	44
1962	36	7	43
1963	35	6	43
1964	33	8	45
1965	33	8	44
1966	33	8	44
1967	32	8	42
1968	33	9	43
1969	30	10	41
1970	30	9	41
1971	30	10	37
1972	32	11	33
1973	28	11	36
1974	32	11	34
1975	29	13	35
1976	28	12	35
1977	30	13	32

Table VII-24
MAGHREB GROUP

INTERNATIONAL TRADE 1950-1977
(Percent)

	EXPORTS TO:		IMPORTS FROM:
Year	U.S. as % of Total Exports	Maghreb Group as % of Total Exports	U.S. as % of Total Imports
1950	2	4	6
1951	2	5	6
1952	2	5	6
1953	2	5	5
1954	2	5	6
1955	2	4	5
1956	1	5	6
1957	1	4	7
1958	1	4	5
1959	2	4	4
1960	1	4	4
1961	1	4	7
1962	1	2	10
1963	1	2	8
1964	1	2	7
1965	1	2	8
1966	1	1	12
1967	1	1	12
1968	1	1	12
1969	1	1	10
1970	1	2	10
1971	2	2	10
1972	6	2	8
1973	9	2	9
1974	16	2	11
1975	20	1	12
1976	33	1	10
1977	41	0	8

Table VII-25
UNION OF CENTRAL AFRICAN STATES (UDEAC):

INTERNATIONAL TRADE 1950-1977
(Percent)

| Year | EXPORTS TO: | | IMPORTS FROM: |
	U.S. as % of Total Exports	UDEAC as % of Total Exports	U.S. as % of Total Imports
1950	2	0	10
1951	5	0	6
1952	6	0	9
1953	9	0	5
1954	10	0	5
1955	11	0	7
1956	8	0	7
1957	6	0	5
1958	6	0	6
1959	10	0	5
1960	5	1	6
1961	4	1	6
1962	6	0	6
1963	8	1	1
1964	10	1	6
1965	13	1	7
1966	15	1	6
1967	15	0	5
1968	12	3	6
1969	7	3	7
1970	6	3	8
1971	7	3	8
1972	8	4	10
1973	7	3	8
1974	15	1	6
1975	18	2	5
1976	15	2	7
1977	15	3	5

Table VII-26
WEST AFRICAN ECONOMIC COMMUNITY (CEAO):

INTERNATIONAL TRADE 1950-1977
(Percent)

Year	EXPORTS TO:		IMPORTS FROM:
	U.S. as % of Total Exports	CEAO as % of Total Exports	U.S. as % of Total Imports
1950	0	0	0
1951	0	0	0
1952	0	0	0
1953	0	0	0
1954	0	0	0
1955	0	0	0
1956	0	0	0
1957	0	0	0
1958	0	0	0
1959	0	0	0
1960	7	1	3
1961	7	2	3
1962	8	4	4
1963	8	3	5
1964	12	41	7
1965	8	6	5
1966	9	5	6
1967	7	7	5
1968	9	7	5
1969	9	5	7
1970	10	6	7
1971	10	9	7
1972	8	10	6
1973	7	10	8
1974	4	9	7
1975	6	10	7
1976	8	7	7
1977	9	0	6

Tables VII 27-41

U.S. Direct Investment in Trading Blocs
(excluding EEC and EFTA). All Industries
and Manufacturing, by bloc, 1950-1977, in
millions of dollars.

Note: Tables on direct investment in EEC and
EFTA are included in text.

Table VII-27
U.S. FOREIGN DIRECT INVESTMENT

IN MANUFACTURING, TOTAL WORLD: 1950-1976
(Millions of dollars and percent)

Year	Reinvested Earnings: Million dollars	Reinvested Earnings: Percent	Capital Outflow	Total Direct Investment
1950	$ 266	58%	$ 192	$ 458
1951	359	64	202	561
1952	397	64	228	625
1953	403	107	-27	376
1954	418	74	148	566
1955	477	68	224	701
1956	533	58	390	923
1957	455	51	432	887
1958	464	63	269	733
1959	581	55	468	1,049
1960	627	44	801	1,428
1961	445	49	462	907
1962	514	42	712	1,226
1963	871	53	774	1,645
1964	934	47	1,034	1,968
1965	895	39	1,525	2,420
1966	918	36	1,611	2,529
1967	845	41	1,224	2,069
1968	1,357	59	946	2,303
1969	1,987	62	1,210	3,197
1970	1,528	55	1,263	2,791
1971	1,796	53	1,564	3,360
1972	2,830	71	1,163	3,993
1973	4,107	69	1,863	5,970
1974	3,936	58	2,861	6,797
1975	3,451	73	1,301	4,752
1976	4,126	82	928	5,054

Source: U.S. Department of Commerce unpublished files.

Table VII-28
U.S. DIRECT INVESTMENT[1]/ (ALL INDUSTRIES)

IN THE OCAM COUNTRIES: 1966-1977[2]/
(Millions of dollars)

	1966	1967	1968	1969	1970	1971	1972	1973	1974	1975	1976	1977
Benin	*	-1	3	-2	*	*	-1	-1	3	2	-1	-3
Burundi	*	*	*	*	*	*	*	*	-1	*	*	*
Central African Empire	*	*	*	1	*	1	*	*	1	0	-1	1
Congo	*	*	2	-1	3	1	-3	*	1	*	-1	*
Gabon	4	3	-2	1	**	**	1	5	17	11	29	-13
Ivory Coast	*	1	1	-2	5	1	-2	1	1	6	**	10
Mali	*	*	*	*	-1	*	1	**	2	-4	-1	*
Mauritius	*	*	*	*	*	*	*	*	*	*	**	*
Niger	*	*	*	*	1	2	2	5	10	9	**	-1
Rwanda	*	*	*	-1	**	*	*	*	1	*	-1	*
Senegal	1	1	1	3	**	**	*	2	-3	-8	-4	1
Togo	*	**	3	1	1	1	*	-1	**	1	**	*
Upper Volta	*	1	*	*	*	*	*	*	1	1	-1	*
Zaire	*	1	2	1	6	16	5	9	10	6	33	-9
All Countries	5	7	10	5	18	25	3	20	44	24	52	-15

* Between -$500,000 and +$500,000.
** Not Available (to avoid disclosure of individual operations.)
1/ Defined as equity and intercompany account outflows to and reinvested earnings in foreign affiliates of U.S. corporations which held at least 25 percent ownership interest prior to 1966 and 10 percent interest in all subsequent years.
2/ Data not available for years prior to 1966.
Source: U.S. Department of Commerce files.

Table VII-29
U.S. DIRECT INVESTMENT[1]/ (ALL INDUSTRIES)

IN THE ANCOM COUNTRIES: 1966-1977[2]/
(Millions of dollars)

Year	Chile	Colombia	Bolivia	Ecuador	Peru	Venezuela	TOTAL
1966	22	27	21	6	58	-44	90
1967	45	24	9	10	55	-45	98
1968	96	38	13	20	37	78	282
1969	-78	53	14	32	23	38	82
1970	-16	10	**	44	-23	53	67
1971	-19	68	**	121	-5	-38	126
1972	-94	-15	-1	46	44	-27	-47
1973	1	-3	-6	-10	93	-121	-46
1974	-154	15	-11	102	118	-246	-176
1975	-113	32	6	-118	326	280	413
1976	9	8	-8	26	155	-379	-189
1977	-39	53	27	-78	47	254	264

* Not available (to avoid disclosure of individual transactions).
1/ Defined as equity and intercompany account outflows to and reinvested earnings in foreign affiliates of U.S. corporations which held at least 25 percent ownership interest prior to 1966 and 10 percent interest in all subsequent years.
2/ Data are not available for previous years.
Source: U.S. Department of Commerce unpublished file.

Table VII-30
U.S. DIRECT INVESTMENT$\underline{1/}$ IN MANUFACTURING:

FOUR ANCOM COUNTRIES, 1950-1976
(Millions of dollars)

Year	Chile	Colombia	Peru	Venezuela
1950	*	9	3	5
1951	4	3	6	5
1952	0	10	-4	6
1953	1	4	0	4
1954	1	11	2	9
1955	1	7	5	14
1956	2	10	2	20
1957	3	2	8	30
1958	2	7	1	27
1959	2	10	3	10
1960	1	14	4	19
1961	5	3	*	16
1962	2	7	8	0
1963	-3	18	18	9
1964	3	24	2	15
1965	8	10	12	26
1966	6	26	26	36
1967	9	10	24	1
1968	2	19	-1	50
1969	2	14	12	29
1970	-1	10	-7	41
1971	-8	54	3	49
1972	4	-3	0	27
1973	-2	30	9	29
1974	-3	42	1	103
1975	4	14	11	47
1976	5	8	2	73

* Between -$500,000 and +$500,000.
1/ Defined as equity and intercompany account outflows
to and reinvested earnings in foreign affiliates of
U.S. corporations which held at least 25 percent ownership interest prior to 1966 and 10 percent interest in
all subsequent years.
Source: Survey of Current Business.

Table VII-31
U.S. DIRECT INVESTMENT[1]/ (ALL INDUSTRIES) IN

THE ASEAN COUNTRIES: 1966-1977[2]/
(Millions of dollars)

Year	Malaysia	Thailand	Singapore	Indonesia	Philippines	TOTAL ASEAN
1966	10	7	-3	-28	50	36
1967	-1	22	1	*	63	85
1968	8	30	14	**	42	94
1969	17	22	21	17	80	157
1970	24	22	29	96	-30	141
1971	29	-22	25	182	23	237
1972	37	22	59	164	-4	278
1973	65	10	93	233	25	426
1974	140	91	90	-91	66	296
1975	70	12	132	911	14	1,139
1976	-10	18	-24	-118	66	-68
1977	106	17	171	-328	96	62

* Between -$500,000 and +$500,000.
** Not available (to avoid disclosure of individual operations).
1/ Defined as equity and intercompany account outflows to and reinvested earnings in foreign affiliates of U.S. corporations which held at least 25 percent ownership interest prior to 1966 and 10 percent interest in all subsequent years.
2/ Data not available.
Source: U.S. Department of Commerce, unpublished files.

Table VII-32
U.S. DIRECT INVESTMENTS' IN MANUFACTURING IN

TWO ASEAN COUNTRIES: 1950-1976
(Millions of dollars)

Year	Philippines	Indonesia
1950	2	3
1951	2	5
1952	*	2
1953	1	2
1954	4	1
1955	2	3
1956	4	2
1957	15	*
1958	12	3
1959	9	1
1960	3	2
1961	-3	**
1962	3	**
1963	20	**
1964	18	**
1965	19	**
1966	27	0
1967	36	1
1968	20	1
1969	41	5
1970	8	4
1971	13	9
1972	-3	7
1973	25	11
1974	42	34
1975	4	31
1976	9	4

* Between -$500,000 and +$500,000.
** Data are unavailable.
1/ Defined as equity and intercompany account outflows
to and reinvested earnings in foreign affiliates of
U.S. corporations which held at least 25 percent ownership interest prior to 1966 and 10 percent interest in
all subsequent years.

Table VII-33
U.S. DIRECT INVESTMENT1/ (All INDUSTRIES)

IN THE CARICOM COUNTRIES, 1966-1977 2/
(Millions of dollars)

Year	Barbados	Belize	British Islands	Guyana	Trinidad & Tobago	Jamaica	TOTAL
1966	1	*	1	**	15	41	56
1967	*	*	*	**	10	42	53
1968	3	1	6	**	8	92	110
1969	*	*	7	**	**	96	101
1970	3	*	**	*	**	116	120
1971	3	*	**	-5	64	111	173
1972	6	1	8	1	19	6	40
1973	2	*	**	**	152	-5	192
1974	*	1	131	**	86	-6	211
1975	-1	1	10	1	87	46	144
1976	1	1	-86	*	65	-78	-97
1977	0	2	22	1	208	0	233

* Between -$500,000 and +$500,000.
** Not available (to avoid disclosure of individual transactions).
1/ Defined as equity and intercompany account outflows to and reinvested earnings in foreign affiliates of U.S. corporations which held at least 25 percent ownership interest prior to 1966 and 10 percent interest in all subsequent years.
2/ Data are not available for previous years.
Source: U.S. Department of Commerce unpublished file.

Table VII-34
U.S. DIRECT INVESTMENT 1/ (ALL INDUSTRIES)

IN THE CACM COUNTRIES: 1966-1977 2/
(Millions of dollars)

Year	Costa Rica	El Salvador	Guatamala	Honduras	Nicaragua	TOTAL
1966	11	4	4	14	9	42
1967	26	4	2	21	3	56
1968	-6	4	9	16	6	29
1969	15	4	6	12	2	39
1970	4	*	8	9	6	27
1971	21	3	4	11	11	50
1972	22	-1	-38	1	-10	-26
1973	2	7	19	0	6	34
1974	30	9	30	23	14	106
1975	8	15	-11	-1	11	22
1976	-66	8	40	-6	-3	-27
1977	18	-4	21	13	12	60

* Between -$500,000 and +$500,000.
1/ Defined as equity and intercompany account outflows to and reinvested earnings in foreign affiliates of U.S. corporations which held at least 25 percent ownership interest prior to 1966 and 10 percent interest in all subsequent years.
2/ Data are not available for previous years.
Source: U.S. Department of Commerce unpublished files.

170

Table VII-35
U.S. DIRECT INVESTMENT⅟ IN MANUFACTURING IN CACM:

EL SALVADOR, 1960-1965
(Millions of dollars)

Year	El Salvador
1960	1
1961	3
1962	4
1963	6
1964	9
1965	16

1/ Defined as equity and intercompany account outflows
to and reinvested earnings in foreign affiliates of U.S.
corporations which held at least 25 percent ownership
interest prior to 1966 (and 10 percent interest in all
subsequent years).
Source: U.S. Department of Commerce unpublished files.

Table VII-36
U.S. DIRECT INVESTMENT[1]/ (ALL INDUSTRIES) IN

THE COUNCIL OF ENTENTE STATES: 1966-1977[2]/
(Millions of dollars)

Year	Benin	Ivory Coast	Niger	Togo	Upper Volta	TOTAL
1966	*	*	*	**	*	*
1967	-1	1	*	**	*	2
1968	3	1	*	3	*	7
1969	-2	-2	*	1	*	-3
1970	*	5	1	1	*	7
1971	*	1	2	1	*	4
1972	-1	-2	2	*	*	-1
1973	-1	1	5	-1	*	4
1974	3	1	10	**	1	15
1975	2	6	9	1	1	19
1976	-1	**	**	**	-1	-2
1977	-3	10	-1	*	*	7

* Between -$500,000 and +$500,000.
** Not available (to avoid disclosure of individual transactions).
1/ Defined as equity and intercompany account out-flows to and reinvested earnings in foreign affiliates of U.S. corporations which held at least 25 percent ownership interest prior to 1966 and 10 percent interest in all subsequent years.
2/ Data are not available for previous years.
Source: U.S. Department of Commerce unpublished files.

Table VII-37
U.S. DIRECT INVESTMENT[1] (ALL INDUSTRIES)

IN THE EACM COUNTRIES: 1966-1977[2]
(Millions of dollars)

Year	Kenya	Tanzania	Uganda	TOTAL
1966	-2	*	*	-2
1967	1	1	*	2
1968	-4	*	2	-2
1969	1	*	*	1
1970	8	1	*	9
1971	1	1	*	2
1972	2	1	1	4
1973	13	3	*	16
1974	17	5	*	22
1975	11	3	1	15
1976	17	-2	-2	13
1977	1	*	3	4

* Between -$500,000 and +$500,000.
1/ Defined as equity and intercompany account outflows
to and reinvested earnings in foreign affiliates of
U.S. corporations which held at least 25 percent
ownership interest prior to 1966 and 10 percent
interest in all subsequent years.
2/ Data are not available for previous years.
Source: U.S. Department of Commerce unpublished files.

Table VII-38
U.S. DIRECT INVESTMENT[1]/ IN MANUFACTURING

THE LAFTA COUNTRIES: 1950-1976[2]/
(Millions of dollars)

Year	Argentina	Brazil	Chile	Colombia	Mexico	Peru	Uruguay	Venezuela	TOTAL excluding Uruguay	TOTAL including Uruguay
1950	12	41	**	9	31	3	4	5	101	105
1951	10	109	4	3	63	6	4	5	200	204
1952	25	120	0	10	15	-4	0	6	172	172
1953	2	-33	1	4	4	0	2	4	-18	-16
1954	17	53	1	11	5	2	-3	10	99	96
1955	16	32	1	7	63	5	1	21	146	147
1956	10	52	2	10	47	2	2	20	153	155
1957	10	56	3	2	41	8	-1	30	150	149
1958	-2	78	2	7	1	1	*	27	114	114
1959	23	56	2	10	17	3	-2	10	121	119
1960	53	81	1	14	38	4	1	19	210	211
1961	88	26	5	3	84	*	**	16	322	322
1962	94	63	2	7	34	8	***	0	208	208
1963	29	47	-3	18	58	18	***	9	176	176
1964	38	4	3	14	110	2	***	15	196	196
1965	111	56	8	10	139	3	***	26	353	353
1966	9	131	6	24	68	26	14	36	300	314
1967	39	53	9	7	89	12	**	7	516	516
1968	52	129	0	12	131	6	**	59	389	389

1969	70	141	3	27	129	8	**	31	409	409
1970	27	176	-1	9	104	5	**	39	359	359
1971	44	152	-8	54	117	3	**	49	411	411
1972	29	330	4	-3	155	0	**	27	542	542
1973	27	492	-2	30	157	9	**	-130	583	583
1974	-31	525	-3	42	371	1	**	103	1,008	1,008
1975	41	509	4	14	270	11	**	47	896	896
1976	131	561	5	8	-217	2	**	73	563	563

* Between -$500,000 and +$500,000.
** Data are not available.
1/ Defined as equity and intercompany account outflows to and reinvested earnings in foreign affiliates of U.S. corporations which held at least 25 percent ownership interest prior to 1966 and 10 percent interest in all subsequent years.
2/ Excludes Bolivia, Ecuador and Paraguay.
Source: U.S. Department of Commerce unpublished file.

Table VII-39
U.S. DIRECT INVESTMENT[1]/ (ALL INDUSTRIES)

IN THE MAGHREB GROUP COUNTRIES: 1966-1977[2]/
(Millions of dollars)

Year	Algeria	Morocco	Tunisia	TOTAL
1966	5	2	-1	6
1967	-2	3	2	3
1968	4	3	*	7
1969	**	2	-1	1
1970	-9	1	1	-7
1971	1	3	1	5
1972	-11	5	-1	7
1973	**	-2	-4	-5
1974	**	-3	-2	-5
1975	-22	1	5	-16
1976	3	3	-2	4
1977	*	4	6	10

* Between -$500,000 and +$500,000.
** Not available (to avoid disclosure of individual transactions).
1/ Defined as equity and intercompany account outflows to and reinvested earnings in foreign affiliates of U.S. corporations which held at least 25 percent ownership interest prior to 1966 and 10 percent interest in all subsequent years.
2/ Data are not available for previous years.
Source: U.S. Department of Commerce unpublished files.

Table VII-40
U.S. DIRECT INVESTMENT[1] (ALL INDUSTRIES)

IN THE UDEAC COUNTRIES: 1966-1977[2]
(Millions of dollars)

Year	Cameroon	Central African Empire	Congo	Gabon	TOTAL
1966	1	*	*	4	5
1967	*	*	*	3	3
1968	-1	*	2	-2	-1
1969	1	1	-1	1	2
1970	*	*	3	**	6
1971	1	1	1	**	6
1972	1	*	-3	1	-1
1973	*	*	*	5	5
1974	1	1	1	17	20
1975	4	**	*	11	16
1976	5	-1	-1	29	33
1977	**	1	*	-13	-10

* Between -$500,000 and +$500,000.
** Not available (to avoid disclosure of individual transactions).
1/ Defined as equity and intercompany account outflows to and reinvested earnings in foreign affiliates of U.S. corporations which held at least 25 percent ownership interest prior to 1966 and 10 percent interest in all subsequent years.
2/ Data are not available for previous years.
Source: U.S. Department of Commerce unpublished files.

Table VII-41
U.S. DIRECT INVESTMENT1/ (ALL INDUSTRIES) IN

THE CEAO COUNTRIES: 1966-19772/
(Millions of dollars)

Year	Benin	Ivory Coast	Mali	Mauritania	Niger	Senegal	Upper Volta	TOTAL
1966	*	*	*	*	*	1	*	1
1967	-1	1	*	*	*	1	*	1
1968	3	1	*	3	*	1	*	8
1969	-2	-2	*	-2	*	3	*	-3
1970	*	5	-1	1	1	**	*	6
1971	*	1	*	*	2	**	*	4
1972	-1	-2	1	**	2	*	*	*
1973	-1	1	**	**	5	2	*	10
1974	3	1	2	1	10	-3	1	14
1975	2	6	-4	*	9	-8	1	6
1976	-1	**	-1	*	**	-4	-1	-7
1977	-3	10	*	1	-1	1	*	8

* Between -$500,000 and +$500,000.
** Not available (to avoid disclosure of individual transactions).
1/ Defined as equity and intercompany account outflows to and reinvested earnings in foreign affiliates of U.S. corporations which held at least 25 percent ownership interest prior to 1966 and 10 percent interest in all subsequent years.
2/ Data are not available for previous years.
Source: U.S. Department of Commerce unpublished files.

Tables VII 42-48

Fees and Royalties Received by U.S. Business
from Enterprises Abroad, 1956,1957, 1960-1977,
by country, in millions of dollars.

Note: See Technical Note, page 35.

Table VII-42
RECEIPTS OF ROYALTIES AND LICENSE FEES

U.S. FIRMS FROM FOREIGN SOURCES: 1956-1957
(Millions of dollars)

	Foreign unaffiliated companies		Foreign affiliates of U.S. Companies	
	1956	1957	1956	1957
Europe				
France	18.6	19.3	11.5	n.a.
Germany	11.8	13.7	13.8	n.a.
Italy	9.4	9.7	3.4	n.a.
Netherlands	3.0	3.1	1.1	n.a.
Belgium	2.2	2.6	2.0	n.a.
Sweden	2.1	2.6	1.2	n.a.
Switzerland	.4	.5	.9	n.a.
Other West Europe	2.8	4.2	2.5	n.a.
Subtotal	50.3	55.7	36.4	40.5
Sterling Area				
United Kingdom	28.6	28.7	22.3	n.a.
Australia	5.1	5.2	7.2	n.a.
Other Sterling Area	3.0	3.7	13.0	n.a.
Subtotal	36.7	37.6	42.5	44.0
Canada	15.7	16.8	49.6	52.3
Latin American Republics				
Mexico	2.7	3.1	8.3	n.a.
Brazil	2.7	3.0	11.5	n.a.
Other	5.0	5.2	55.2	n.a.
Subtotal	10.4	11.3	75.0	73.0
Other countries				
Japan	11.8	14.9	3.8	n.a.
Other	3.5	4.1	21.2	n.a.
Subtotal	15.3	19.0	25.0	28.1
All Countries	128.4	140.4	228.5	237.9

n.a. Not Available

Table VII-43
TOTAL U.S. RECEIPTS OF FEES AND ROYALTIES

FROM AFFILIATED AND UNAFFILIATED FOREIGN SOURCES,

ALL INDUSTRY AND MANUFACTURING: 1960-1977
(Millions of dollars)

Year	Affiliated (All Industry)	Affiliated (Manufacturing)	Unaffiliated (All Industry)
1960	590	n.a.	247
1961	662	n.a.	244
1962	800	n.a.	256
1963	890	n.a.	273
1964	1,013	n.a.	301
1965	1,199	n.a.	335
1966	1,162	632	353
1967	1,354	706	393
1968	1,430	781	437
1969	1,533	841	486
1970	1,758	944	573
1971	1,927	1,036	618
1972	2,115	1,208	655
1973	2,513	1,552	712
1974	3,070	1,886	751
1975	3,543	2,098	757
1976	3,531	2,100	822
1977	3,767	n.a.	958

n.a.   Not Available

Table VII-44

U.S. RECEIPTS OF FEES AND ROYALTIES FROM

AFFILIATED ASEAN SOURCES

ALL INDUSTRY AND MANUFACTURING: 1966-1977

(Millions of dollars)

Year	Indonesia (All Industry)	Mfg.	Philippines (All Industry)	Mfg.	Malaysia (All Industry)	Singapore (All Industry)	Thailand (All Industry)	TOTAL (All Industry)
1966	3	*	14	5	3	1	**	21
1967	3	*	14	6	3	1	4	25
1968	6	*	15	6	3	4	6	34
1969	9	*	17	6	3	4	6	39
1970	19	1	16	6	3	5	7	50
1971	28	*	16	7	4	8	7	63
1972	25	1	16	6	6	8	7	62
1973	27	2	17	8	7	18	7	76
1974	25	3	19	11	8	12	9	73
1975	34	4	20	11	8	22	10	94
1976	40	4	24	14	11	19	12	106
1977	42	***	24	***	*	10	12	88

* Between -$500,000 and +$500,000.
** Not available (to avoid disclosure of individual transactions).
*** Not available.

Table VII-45
U.S. RECEIPTS OF FEES AND ROYALTIES

FROM AFFILIATED SOURCES IN CARICOM, ALL INDUSTRY: 1966-1977
(Millions of dollars)

Year	Barbados	Belize	British Islands	Guyana	Trinidad & Tobago	Jamaica	TOTAL
1966	*	*	-1	*	2	5	7
1967	*	*	*	*	4	6	11
1968	*	*	*	*	4	7	12
1969	*	*	*	1	2	9	14
1970	*	*	*	*	2	13	17
1971	*	*	*	*	3	15	20
1972	*	*	*	*	4	16	24
1973	*	*	*	*	2	13	19
1974	1	*	1	*	4	13	24
1975	1	*	2	*	4	15	31
1976	1	*	2	*	5	9	27
1977	1	*	1	*	5	5	23

* Between -$500,000 and +$500,000.

Table VII-46

U.S. RECEIPTS OF FEES AND ROYALTIES FROM AFFILIATED COMPANIES

IN THE CACM COUNTRIES, ALL INDUSTRY: 1966-1977

	Costa Rica	El Salvador	Guatemala	Honduras	Nicaragua	TOTAL
1966	1	1	2	1	*	5
1967	2	1	4	1	1	9
1968	5	1	2	2	1	11
1969	2	1	3	1	3	10
1970	2	1	1	2	2	8
1971	5	1	3	3	1	14
1972	6	2	4	3	1	15
1973	5	3	2	2	2	12
1974	8	2	3	2	2	18
1975	7	2	3	4	2	16
1976	5	3	3	4	2	16
1977	5	3	4	5	3	20

*Between -$500,000 and +$500,000.

Table VII-47

U.S. RECEIPTS OF FEES AND ROYALTIES FROM AFFILIATED

MANUFACTURING SOURCES IN THE EEC COUNTRIES: 1966-1976

(Millions of dollars)

Year	Belgium & Luxembourg	France	Germany	Italy	Nether-lands	United Kingdom	Denmark	Ireland
1966	14	50	63	24	24	108	1	1
1967	17	46	60	29	25	133	2	1
1968	22	52	68	35	32	136	2	1
1969	27	60	83	39	34	152	4	1
1970	37	56	93	51	47	164	3	2
1971	41	75	107	54	41	172	3	1
1972	48	98	129	57	47	193	3	1
1973	68	132	184	83	60	234	4	4
1974	91	149	215	115	75	266	4	5
1975	105	201	238	118	70	335	4	13
1976	105	166	240	115	81	312	6	17

Table VII-48

U.S. RECEIPTS OF FEES AND ROYALTIES FROM AFFILIATED

MANUFACTURING SOURCES IN SELECTED LAFTA COUNTRIES: 1966-1976
(Millions of dollars)

Year	Argentina	Brazil	Chile	Colombia	Mexico	Peru	Venezuela
1966	15	10	1	4	33	3	7
1967	16	7	2	3	42	7	9
1968	19	8	2	6	49	8	11
1969	17	8	2	6	47	3	10
1970	18	7	2	6	52	3	11
1971	15	7	2	3	51	4	15
1972	15	9	2	3	58	4	15
1973	12	9	1	6	73	4	18
1974	10	9	3	2	86	4	12
1975	7	5	1	5	99	3	11
1976	8	7	1	5	76	1	8

Tables VII 49-52

New Licensing Agreements of U.S. Business
with Foreign Enterprise, 1961-1974, by
Country (number of agreements).

Note: See Technical Note, Page 35.

Table VII-49
NEW LICENSING ACTIVITY

OF U.S. FIRMS OVERSEAS
(Number of agreements)

1961	340
1962	247
1963	304
1964	282
1965	259
1966	174
1967	139
1968	133
1969	177
1970	129
1971	113
1972	128
1973	117
TOTAL	2,542

Table VII-50

NEW LICENSING ACTIVITIES OF U.S. FIRMS IN

SELECTED AREAS AND COUNTRIES
(Number of agreements)

	Japan	Canada	Australia	Oceania	India	Asia (excluding Japan)	Africa	Western Hemisphere (excluding Canada)
FY 1961	63	19	13	16	8	27	12	50
FY 1962	50	19	12	12	5	16	5	39
FY 1963	48	32	13	16	8	17	12	46
FY 1964	79	25	14	15	5	14	10	33
FY 1965	56	16	12	15	13	22	9	36
CY 1969	62	5	10	10	--	8	2	18
CY 1970	30	1	2	4	1	24	4	19
CY 1971	46	3	2	3	1	3	--	9
CY 1972	49	1	5	5	--	5	2	12
CY 1973	54	6	5	7	1	10	1	2

FY: Fiscal Year, July 1 through June 30.
CY: Calendar Year.

Table VII-51

NEW LICENSING ACTIVITIES OF

U.S. FIRMS IN THE EEC COUNTRIES AND WESTERN EUROPE

1961-1965, 1969-1973
(Number of agreements)

	Belgium-Luxembourg	France	Italy	Netherlands	Germany	TOTAL EEC	Western Europe
FY 1961	4	20	17	5	27	73	136
FY 1962	7	19	8	7	21	62	123
FY 1963	7	10	19	9	18	63	115
FY 1964	4	14	9	5	18	50	123
FY 1965	3	22	13	6	16	60	115
CY 1969	5	5	17	4	9	40	72
CY 1970	1	6	3	3	10	23	47
CY 1971	2	9	3	-	11	25	49
CY 1972	2	4	8	1	10	25	54
CY 1973	1	3	6	1	8	19	37

FY: Fiscal Year July 1 through June 30.
CY: Calendar Year.

Table VII-52

NEW LICENSING ACTIVITIES OF U.S. FIRMS

IN THE EFTA COUNTRIES AND WESTERN EUROPE

1961-1965, 1969-1973
(Number of agreements)

	Switzerland	United Kingdom	Sweden	Other EFTA	TOTAL EFTA	Western Europe
FY 1961	2	46	5	3	56	136
FY 1962	2	48	5	3	56	123
FY 1963	2	32	7	5	46	115
FY 1964	5	53	6	3	67	123
FY 1965	-	38	6	1	45	115
CY 1969	2	19	3	3	27	72
CY 1970	4	11	3	2	20	47
CY 1971	1	12	1	1	15	54
CY 1972	1	7	5	2	15	54
CY 1973	1	7	1	-	9	37

FY: Fiscal Year, July 1 through June 30.
CY: Calendar Year.

Index